DR. FORMAT

ANSWERS YOUR QUESTIONS

Revised Edition

by David Trottier

Second Applewood Arts Edition
10 9 8 7 6 5 4 3

Library of Congress Cataloging-in-Publication Data

Trottier, David
Dr. Format Answers Your Questions, Revised Edition / by
David Trottier
p. cm.
Includes index.
1. Motion picture authorship. 2. Television authorship.
I. Title
808.2'3   2002093850 LCCN

ISBN: 978-1-885655-07-3

Cover design by Bob Nicholl

Printed in the United States of America

Applewood Arts
4456 Manchester St.
Cedar Hills, UT 84062

PURPOSE AND CONTENTS

The purpose of this book is to provide you with guidance on very specific formatting and spec screenplay writing topics. Understanding formatting and spec writing is a necessary **key** to crafting a readable and saleable script. This book shows you how to turn the key. **I suggest you read it from cover to cover** for a thorough review of spec writing principles. There will naturally be some overlap of explanations.

This book contains two main sections:

1. A newly **updated** version of all of my *Dr. Format* **columns** published in *Script* magazine from 1997 to 2008, plus two articles on screenwriting.

2. A clear and thorough **index**, beginning on page 217. Use this index as a reference guide to find explanations of every possible formatting situation.

For information concerning my services, books, and freebies, or *Script* magazine, see page 229.

Keep writing,
Dave Trottier
www.keepwriting.com
dave@keepwriting.com

DR. FORMAT COLUMNS
Script magazine
1997 to 2008

plus two articles on screenwriting

First Dr. Format Column
February, 1997

It seems like every week I come across some new rule that someone is touting as the latest in script format. I get regular calls from writers asking about this fine point or that.

This column will answer your formatting questions. In doing so, I hope to take the mystery out of formatting, dispel the confusion that surrounds it, explode common formatting myths, and help you make that all-important first impression with your script.

What is the point?
The purpose of formatting is to present a story in readable form so that the reader will recommend your script to higher-ups. *Readable form* means the reader can easily visualize the action of the story, hear the characters in his or her head, and feel the emotion that underpins the story. That means the writing must be clear, moving, and easy-to-follow.

Some writers believe this means including camera angles, editing instructions, and other technical directions. This is exactly the wrong thing to do. Why? Because it intrudes on "the read." Which is more interesting to read? *ESTABLISHING SHOT - NEW YORK* or *The skyline of New York City sparkles in the sunlight.* The second version is clearer, more easily visualized, and easier to read.

Another purpose of formatting is to provide a generally-accepted standard framework in which to tell a story, not direct the movie. That constantly-evolving standard includes three basic sections: 1) Headings, including the master scene heading, 2) Narrative description, and 3) Dialogue. You are familiar with these, but do you understand the fine points of formatting that make a difference?

Formatting is not one of the profundities of the universe. It is simple and straight-forward. On the other hand, formatting is more than just a few rules about margins and tabs, it is a style guide to writing a salable script. To understand formatting is to understand screenwriting.

WORKING WITH FOREIGN LANGUAGES

QUESTION
If I have a conversation in Chinese as well as English, do I use the dreaded wrylies to define Chinese and English? Also, in defining film reality, can I avoid the language barrier by writing my Chinese scenes in English?

ANSWER
First, let me explain the question. The writer refers to "dreaded wrylies." *Wrylies* are the parentheticals that sometimes appear before dialogue. The term developed because so many beginners used the term *wryly* to describe their characters' dialogue.

```
                    JOHN
              (wryly)
      The night is still young,
      Cupcake.
```

And so the term *wryly* was born. The reason they are "dreaded" is because writers are encouraged to limit their use. Only use a wryly when the subtext of the dialogue is not otherwise clear. You can also use wrylies to briefly describe a character's action while he speaks.

In working with other languages, realize there is one central principle: Write your script in the language of the eventual reader. If a character speaks in Chinese, do not write the dialogue out in Chinese characters unless the eventual reader is Chinese. Simply write the line as follows.

```
                  JOHN
             (in Chinese)
        The night is still young,
        Cupcake.
```

If the characters speak in Chinese throughout an entire scene, then make a clear statement in the narrative description that all the dialogue in the scene will be spoken in Chinese; then, write it out in English so the reader can understand it.

But this begs the question: How will the audience know what is being said? They won't. That's why one option is to write a line or two in Chinese for flavor, and otherwise allow the characters to speak in English so that the audience will understand what is going on.

There is another alternative—subtitles. If you want English subtitles to appear on the screen while the characters speak in Chinese, then include a special note in the narrative description.

```
NOTE:  The dialogue in this scene is
spoken in Chinese with English subtitles.
```

Then, simply write the dialogue out in English. After the scene ends, write:

```
END OF SUBTITLES
```

See pages 86-87 for other ways to indicate subtitles.

A SUPER QUESTION

QUESTION
When writing a screenplay, is it the writer who writes the text that appears on the screen? I'm thinking of *X-files* and *Clear and Present Danger*.

ANSWER
The *text* you refer to is actually a SUPERIMPOSITION. You *superimpose* a title card or *legend* over the image that we see. The term *superimpose* is generally shortened to SUPER in a spec script. Here's an example.

```
EXT. HOSPITAL - NIGHT

EMTs rush a patient out of an ambulance
and into the hospital.

SUPER: "Bethesda Medical Hospital."

Scully's car comes to a quick stop.  She
steps out with her cellular.

                    SCULLY
                (into cellular)
          Mulder?  Are you there?
```

Please note that I followed the heading (or slug line) with a sentence of description. I want to first give the audience a visual image before presenting the SUPER that will appear over that image.

If you'd like, here is an alternative expression for a SUPER:

```
The words "BETHESDA MEDICAL HOSPITAL"
spell out across the lower left of the
screen.
```

THE UNKINDEST "CUT TO" OF ALL

QUESTION
Someone told me, "If I submit my script using the CUT TO editing direction like William Goldman does, my script is going to get laughed straight into the trash can." On the other hand, some screenwriting books promote the use of CUT TO. Is there a proper time and place for CUT TO, or should I omit the use of the term altogether?

ANSWER
First of all, established writers can do what they please and Goldman (one of my heroes) uses the CUT TO after virtually every scene. But that's excessive by spec script standards.

Although a screenwriting book may recommend use of the CUT TO, it will not suggest that you use it a la William Goldman. However, in the evolution of *spec* format, the CUT TO is seldom used today. Look at the copyright notice of any book recommending its use and note how long it's been since that book was written; also, make sure the book is not demonstrating *shooting* script format.

In writing a *spec* script today, avoid editing directions like CUT TO, DISSOLVE TO, WIPE TO, MATCH CUT, etc. However, there are times to use them. Here is Trottier Axiom #7 to guide you: *Use an editing direction when it is absolutely necessary to understand the story, or when its use helps link two scenes in a way that creates humor or improves continuity.* Under that rule of thumb, I find myself using editing directions about twice every 120 pages.

In the following example, Bruno stands next to a bed with a canopy overhead. Lying on the bed is Alice. Bruno has resisted her verbal advances up until now, so she tries a new approach.

                         ALICE
             Here, let me give you a
             little candy sampler of
             what's waiting for you on
             the honeymoon.

She swings her legs up, throws a scissors
lock around Bruno's neck and flips him
onto the bed, then pounces on him like a
professional wrestler. His eyes grow
wide in terror.

                                        CUT TO:

INT. BEDROOM - THE NEXT MORNING

Bruno's leg dangles from the canopy. He
blissfully sings an Italian love song.

Alice, below him, lays back on the bed
with her hands behind her head, calmly
smoking a cigar.

The purpose of the CUT TO here is to provide continuity
between the two scenes. The CUT TO also sets up the visual
punch line--it links the *before* with the *after*. Thus, we have a
special *story* reason to use it.

Keep in mind that in virtually all scene transitions, one scene
ends, followed by the heading for the next scene. The CUT
TO is nearly always understood to be there and does not need
to be written. In short, let the editor do the editing and you do
the writing.

SING FOR YOUR SUPPER

QUESTION
I am currently polishing a script that includes old song lyrics and improvisational rap in the dialogue. The parenthetical direction (i.e., rapping, singing) will probably work in most cases, but seems overused because of the volume of lyrical dialogue. I am considering four formatting options: 1) italicizing the lyrics, 2) underscoring, 3) using poetry-style layout (as opposed to wraparound text), and 4) slash marks (/) to convey lyrical rhythm. I can't seem to find a formatting rule to cover this. Help!

ANSWER
The reason you cannot find a formatting rule is because you are not supposed to include songs in a spec script. It's best not to quote any songs to which you don't own the rights. Doing so creates a possible legal roadblock to selling your script because the producer must obtain the rights to use the songs.

If the song is in the public domain, then you may use the lyrics. However, resist the temptation of using a song in a script unless the song has a powerful *story* purpose. When an agent or producer sees song lyrics in a script, they generally react negatively.

If the songs (or "improvisational rap") are original to you, including them in your script still adds an obstacle to the selling process. It means that the producer must not only love your script but the music/lyrics you wrote for it as well. And maybe he or she will.

If you must include song lyrics, use the parentheticals you mention, and place the lyrics in stanza format (your #3 in your question) or use slash marks (your #4) to separate the lines. The following is by Ogden Nash.

```
                         OG
                   (rapping)
          I don't think I'll ever see/
          A billboard lovely as a tree/
          Indeed, the tree I'll not see
          at all/ If the billboard
          doesn't fall.
```

Remember that a spec script should focus primarily on a great story. Tell a great story, and you'll be singing all the way to the bank.

DAYDREAM BELIEVER

QUESTION
If a character is listening to someone talking, and the character drifts off into a daydream or fantasy, how do you set it up?

ANSWER
Handle this the way you would a flashback. First, create a transitional device to slip us into the daydream. In the *Casablanca* flashback, we move toward the cigarette smoke and DISSOLVE to Paris. But a transition could easily be signaled with a word of dialogue or an action. Here's an example.

```
Mary listens to the voices behind the
door.  They fade as she looks away.

MARY'S DAYDREAM
```

Describe the daydream. Then:

```
BACK TO SCENE
```

And continue with the original scene with Mary at the door.

If you have a special location in mind that you want to emphasize, write it as follows:

```
INT. AFRICAN JUNGLE -- MARY'S DAYDREAM
```

Or

```
MARY'S DAYDREAM -- AFRICAN JUNGLE
```

And then after the scene ends:

```
END OF DAYDREAM
```

```
INT. HALLWAY
```

...Or wherever the original scene took place.

Keep in mind that a spec script must be visually clear. The reader must be able to easily visualize the action and movement.

HOW WIDE IS A LINE?

QUESTION
I recently bought formatting software. The dialogue width (between the left margin of the speech and the right margin of the speech] seems to be wider than in most screenplays I've purchased and read. Can you tell me how wide a line of dialogue should be before it wraps around to the next line? It seems about 32-36 characters is proper width, but I've read it should be much shorter.

ANSWER
The ideal is three inches, but you can stretch that to about 3½ inches max. That gives you a range of about 30-35 characters

per line (assuming you are using a standard 10 characters-per-inch font such as Courier or New Courier 12 point).

EXECUTIVE READERS AND READER READERS

QUESTION
I've read that executives and readers don't read narrative description, only dialogue. Is this accurate? If so, what's the best way to convey the action of the screenplay?

ANSWER
You have named two very different types of readers. A *reader* reader (the official term is *story analyst*) is someone who is paid (usually a pittance) to read scripts and write coverages. A *coverage* consists of a two-page synopsis (approximately) plus an evaluation of the script, along with the story analyst's recommendations. In order to write the coverage, the story analyst (reader) must read the script. So generally speaking, a professional reader reads both the narrative description and the dialogue.

An executive, agent or producer usually does not read a script until he has a coverage. If the coverage is favorable, he may read the script, or portions thereof, to see if he agrees with the opinion of the reader. Some Hollywood types read dialogue only, some read just a few pages, and some read the script like a professional reader. Some have law backgrounds or otherwise have little experience with screenplay form. Others have been in the business their entire lives.

In any case, you want to write narrative that's lean. When any reader sees big blocks of black ink, he or she is likely to black out. You want to write description that presents clear images and clear actions. Only include what is necessary to move the story forward.   As a general rule, paragraphs of narration should not exceed four lines.   And, as a very general guideline, each paragraph should focus on one main image or one beat of action.

Let's examine the following poorly written narrative.

EXT. TRAIN - DAY

We see the skyline of New York from a train. Painted on the side of it are words that say, Brooklyn Railroad. It's going very fast and has a gray look to it.

INT. TRAIN - DAY

Inside the train are all kinds of commuters. They are from every age and ethnic group and they fill the train car clean up. They are all headed to work in New York City as can be plainly seen from their working clothes. A bunch of them cannot find seats and must stand. One of them is SALLY STANWICK, who has piercing blue eyes and long, flowing locks of blonde hair. She is in her mid twenties and is wearing a silk blouse with a pink sweater over it and a plain black cotton skirt. She senses someone behind her and turns to see a young man giving her the eye and smiling at her in a very peculiar way.

Here we have the first two paragraphs of a screenplay written by one of my clients (before he became a client). Let's whittle them down while describing specific images and actions.

```
FADE IN:

A speeding silver train races down the
tracks towards Manhattan.

A sign on the train reads: "BROOKLYN
RAILROAD."

INT. TRAIN - DAY

Working professionals crowd the train
car. Some stand.

Among them is SALLY STANWICK, 25, pretty
in a simple cotton dress.  She turns
abruptly, sensing someone's stares.

A young man in a suit greets her with a
smug smile.
```

Now this is not brilliant writing, but it serves our purposes. The first two images are the train and sign, establishing departure location and destination. The third image is of the people in the train car. The fourth paragraph describes a character and her action. And the fifth describes the actions of the second character.

Please note that I omit Sally's eye and hair color to keep casting options open. I omit the specifics of her clothes because they are irrelevant. I give her a simple cotton dress as a way to comment on her character—this is an uncomplicated young woman.

In a word, make sure your dialogue and narrative description are lean and move the story forward. Doing so will help your career move forward as well.

HEADINGS AND MASTER SCENES

QUESTION
I have sequences in which several scenes occur in different rooms of the same building. Right now the scene headings read something like this:

INT. BUILDING/JOE'S APARTMENT/LIVING ROOM

INT. BUILDING/CORRIDOR OUTSIDE JOE'S ROOM

INT. BUILDING/GARAGE

Some books say the above is proper form, but you seem to suggest otherwise in *The Screenwriter's Bible*.

ANSWER
What you have written would be fine if you replaced the slashes with dashes, although you're missing two things.

1. The time. Does this scene take place in the day or night (for example, INT. BUILDING - DAY)? Remember the reader must be oriented to three things in a scene: Where the camera is (INT. or EXT.), location, and time (usually DAY or NIGHT).

2. Readability. The example is a bit difficult to read. That's why I suggest an alternative that I believe makes the script easier to read.

First set up a master scene, then cut to smaller locations contained within that master location.

In the example below, we begin with a master scene heading, then move to locations within that master scene location by using secondary headings.

```
INT. APARTMENT BUILDING - DAY
```

```
IN JOE'S APARTMENT
```

```
AT THE REFRIGERATOR
```

```
THE CORRIDOR OUTSIDE THE APARTMENT
```

All of these secondary locations can be found within the master location, the apartment building. Once we're out of the apartment building, establish a new master scene. The main thing is to make the script readable without losing the reader.

ACTION AND SCENE HEADINGS

I've been editing a sequence in a script of mine, and wondered just how I should go about designating scene headings in a dogfight; i.e., a battle between planes (or tanks, or spaceships), with cuts to inside individual vehicles and back to the battlefield itself. I'm talking about sequences like those in TOP GUN or STAR WARS (whose scripts I'd consult if I could find them).

[Let me (Dave) interject here that there are many businesses that sell scripts. Just keep in mind when you buy a script that it is likely a *shooting script*, while you are writing a *spec script* (written on speculation that you'll sell it later), so avoid the camera directions and technical intrusions you normally see in shooting scripts.]

Right now, things in my script look roughly like this:

```
EXT. SKY ABOVE THE MEDITERRANEAN - DAY
```

```
An enemy plane gets behind Johnny's
fighter.
```

INT. EAGLE TWO

Jimmy looks to his right at EAGLE ONE.

> JIMMY
> Look out, Johnny!

EXT. SKY

Eagle One dodges and weaves while the enemy fires at him.

> JIMMY (V.O.)
> He's on your tail!

INT. EAGLE ONE

Johnny pulls up on the stick.

> JOHNNY
> Thanks for the tip!

QUESTION 1
Would you treat the entire battle as one master scene?

ANSWER
Actually, what you have written above looks fine to me, at least in terms of formatting. On the other hand, you could treat the battle as a master scene with a master scene heading followed by several secondary headings. In that case, the sequence might contain the following scene headings:

EXT. SKY ABOVE THE MEDITERRANEAN - DAY

INSIDE EAGLE TWO

JUST ABOVE THE WATER

```
OUTSIDE ENEMY FIGHTER

INSIDE EAGLE ONE

OUTSIDE EAGLE TWO
```

The key is not so much to be technically correct, but to be clear and readable. As long as the reader can easily visualize what you are describing, then you'll be okay.

QUESTION 2
How would you indicate time during the battle? Would you put "SAME" after each scene heading?

ANSWER
You could if it is not otherwise obvious that these scenes all take place at the same time. In this case, I think the reader would naturally assume that we are in the *same* moment of time and that this is one battle and one main battle location.

QUESTION 3
Am I missing any other elements in making this rather complicated sequence comprehensible?

ANSWER
If you cross-cut between two locations (back and forth), consider using the INTERCUT.

One important key in writing headings is to be clear and accurate, not clever or cute.

Questions for this section were submitted by Chris DelliCarpini.

GETTING DOWN TO BRASS BRADS

QUESTION
Although the script is three-hole punched, do I only use two brads? And what size brads do I use?

ANSWER
It is fashionable to leave the middle hole without a brad and only use two brads. I use ACCO No. 5 Brass Fasteners. They are 1 1/4" in length. I like ACCO because they are sturdier than the more flimsy brads I've seen elsewhere. ACCO pays me nothing to say this.

Some writers wonder why producers and agents prefer brass brads to more permanent forms of binding, such as a spiral binding. Many readers like to read loose pages. In addition, if a producer likes your script, he or she will rip out the two brass brads and photocopy it to show to others in the company (to solicit their opinions). If your script is permanently bound, it cannot be easily photocopied.

MUSIC AND SONG TITLES

QUESTION
While I do not score the screenplay by naming specific songs, may I write something like DRAMATIC MUSIC PLAYS? If the character turns on the radio, may I write, "Jason flips on the radio, which plays 'Do You Believe in Magic?' by the Lovin' Spoonful"?

ANSWER
Generally, you should not name a specific song title unless you control the rights to that song. When you list a specific song title, the producer believes that only that song will make the story work (otherwise, why would you list it?), and if you

don't have rights to the song, then the producer will have to secure them. That may (or may not) be a selling obstacle.

Seldom do you indicate music in the script. Your job is to write a clear and compelling story. If you've established mood and subtext through your excellent writing, then the director and music composer will know when and where to insert the music, and what kind of music to compose.

Indicate music generically: "Jason flips on the radio, which plays an upbeat sixties tune." That's the safe route. You may get away with this: "The radio plays a Lovin' Spoonful-type song." You might even get away with adding, "…such as 'Do You Believe in Magic?'" You're still leaving the choice open. However, only try this once or so in a script, if at all. Remember, it's the story that sells, not the musical selections. So focus on story.

CREDITS AND TITLES

QUESTION
Do I write ROLL CREDITS?

ANSWER
No. There is no need to. The director and producer will make that decision. Often, when a writer indicates credits, he or she demonstrates his or her ignorance. How long should the credits roll? How do you make that judgment, for example, with opening credits? You would need to write CREDITS ROLL and then you'd have to indicate at some point END CREDITS. Don't mess with this stuff.

Just write the story in specific language so that the reader sees, hears, and feels. That's your job.

WHEN THE COMPUTER SPEAKS

QUESTION
I am writing a script which has a dialogue situation between two people via e-mail. Thus, from a computer user's POV, he types an answer to another person's e-mailed question. The answer then appears on the computer user's monitor and so on. Do I write this just as if they were actually speaking the words, or do I do something like this in narrative description: John sees the answer on the screen and responds, "Blah, blah, blah."

Or, if I write it as dialogue, should I preface this dialogue sequence with something like this: "The following conversation appears on John's monitor from his POV."

ANSWER
First of all, only words that are spoken should appear as dialogue. That is what dialogue is. However, if a person repeats out loud what she reads on the monitor, then you could write what she actually says as dialogue.

Otherwise, you will want to find a clear way that doesn't confuse the reader or slow down the read. Perhaps, something like this:

John faces his computer monitor, then begins typing on the keyboard.

ON JOHN'S MONITOR

the words appear:

          "But Renee, they're tapping
          my phone conversations."

BACK TO JOHN

```
who studies Renee's response, then
chuckles.

ON JOHN'S MONITOR

Renee's response appears:

          "You're being silly, John."
```

This is just one of many ways to handle email and texting (and please note that you should indent the words that are typed, just as if they *were* dialogue).

Avoid using POV or other such camera angles. The reason I like the above is because it's easy to read and absolutely clear what is happening. However, it does take a lot of space, so there might be a way to shorten it (perhaps omitting the phase "the words appear" and "Renee's response appears").

A CAST OF THOUSANDS

QUESTION
How would you refer to characters who are "cannon fodder"; i.e., the numerous anonymous characters who may have one line?   At some point, the simple description fails; e.g., COMPUTER TECHNICIAN #27. Would you give them all names for the sake of simplicity, even though they'll never be called by their names?

ANSWER
It's hard to imagine a script with 27 technicians, all with speaking parts. To be honest, I've never seen that many anonymous characters in a script that was sold, optioned, or produced. That's because writers try to give the dialogue to the main characters.

As a general rule, you should only give names to major and minor characters that are "important."

Characters with only one or two lines *may* be given names, but usually *aren't* given names so that the reader knows not to focus on them. (You see, a reader may feel that he must keep track of any characters who have names, especially early in the script.) So instead, refer to these unimportant characters in a way that makes them easy to visualize or distinguish: GRUFF TECH, SEXY TECH, NOSE-RINGED GEEK, and so on.

Let me summarize with another example.

If you have six police officers speaking in a scene (POLICEMAN 1, POLICEMAN 2, and so on), my first reaction is to recommend that you reduce the number of speaking police officers to one or two.

If any of these six officers is an important character, try to give him/her most of the lines. If these officers are not important (have no lines, or have just one or two lines, or only appear in one or two scenes), I would distinguish them in some visual way that *characterizes* them: MACHO COP, TOOTH PICK, TWITCHY COP, etc. This makes them easier to visualize and signals to the reader that they are not particularly important.

BEING FANCY IS CHANCY

QUESTION
Should I include special effects sketches or story boards with my script?

ANSWER
No. The reader wants a script that tells a story. Do not include drawings, sketches, story boards, fancy title pages, special binding, special fonts, bold typeface, italic typeface, etc. Just present a well-written, emotionally satisfying story that we can visualize, written in correct spec format.

SCREEN SPLITTING

QUESTION
In my current script, a man and a woman compete for one job opening. They are treated very differently by the boss and co-workers on their respective first days of work. I would like to show the difference using a SPLIT SCREEN as opposed to an INTERCUT, or a straight-forward presentation of one scene and then the next.

Can you recommend a format that, as the scene progresses over 2-3 pages, would keep the action clear?

While the action/dialogue proceeds on one side of the screen, how would you address the "dead time" on the other side of the screen? Would quick back and forth between screens address that problem? I also thought of starting with a SPLIT SCREEN that then alternately WIPES or ROLLS into a FULL SCREEN to show just the action/dialogue on that side.

ANSWER
I see several problems with your proposal.

First, running two scenes simultaneously on the screen could easily confuse the audience and pull them right out of the movie. The best effects don't call attention to themselves, but to the story.

Second, you mention problems with "dead time," and solving those by WIPING and ROLLING to FULL SCREEN. Do you see that you are creating problems by using the SPLIT SCREEN device in the first place?

Third, I worry that you might be getting more involved in directing the movie than writing it. In those few movies that have used a SPLIT SCREEN, it usually became part of the style for the whole movie. In other words, the device was not used only once. Also, it is usually only used for telephone conversations and, as such, is usually formatted just like the INTERCUT.

If you decide to go ahead anyway because you have an overriding story reason to use this technique, you are probably going to have to split several pages of your screenplay; in other words, you'd have to write the scenes side-by-side in two columns. You would also have to CUT or WIPE to full screen on occasion. Just write it that way.

My recommendation, however, is to avoid using a SPLIT SCREEN...and keep writing

AND THE REST IS HISTORY

QUESTION
I am presently working on a screenplay about the local history. How can I get a quick copyright on my idea just in case someone else stumbles on to what I am writing about?

ANSWER
History and ideas cannot usually be copyrighted. You cannot protect ideas, premises, titles, etc. You can only protect your original expression of an idea—your screenplay.

History is in the public domain, meaning that it belongs to everyone. However, you cannot base your screenplay on an historical book without getting the rights to that book.

Finally, if the local history you refer to is recent and not well-known, you may need to get the rights to the story from the participants.

LEGAL NOTE: This question and all legal questions should be addressed to a competent entertainment attorney. I am not an attorney, and nothing in this book should be construed as legal advice.

MOVIE CLIPS

QUESTION
How do I write out my opening scene if I'm using a clip from another movie?

ANSWER
You cannot use a clip from another movie unless you control the rights to that movie. Do not open your screenplay with a scene from an existing movie. Do not base your screenplay on any work that you do not control the rights to. Do not write the sequel to SNOW WHITE unless you control the rights to SNOW WHITE. Just write an original screenplay.

Obviously, you may briefly refer to other movies in dialogue if doing so moves the story forward or adds to character. For example, in SLEEPLESS IN SEATTLE, there are references to THE DIRTY DOZEN and AN AFFAIR TO REMEMBER. But don't write, "He turned on the TV and the sinking scene from TITANIC was playing." Doing that will give you a sinking feeling when your script is rejected.

VERBS, ADJECTIVES, AND WISDOM

QUESTION
Dr. Format, you often talk about using specific verbs to describe actions without adverbs, and using specific nouns without using adjectives. Are you saying that adjectives and adverbs should be avoided whenever possible?

ANSWER
No, I'm saying that you won't need to use nearly as many adjectives and adverbs if you use specific, concrete nouns and verbs.

For example, here's a sentence containing an adverb and adjective: *He ran quickly to the little house.* Here is the same sentence, using a concrete verb and a concrete noun: *He raced to the cottage.* Because I am using concrete language, I do not need the adverb and adjective.

However, even when you use concrete nouns and verbs, you still may see a need for concrete adjectives and adverbs. In the following sentence, I add a couple of adjectives for visual clarification: *He raced to the red brick bungalow.* Thus, my real point is this: Use concrete, visual language in your narrative description.

The late, great Paddy Cheyvsky (*Marty, Network*), once said, "I have two rules. First, cut out all the wisdom; then, cut out all the adjectives." I don't think he means he actually goes through the script and omits every adjective; I believe he is referring to lean, concrete language. The "cutting out all the wisdom" alludes to the tendency for some scripts to become preachy, or overstate their theme, or write pretentious, unnatural dialogue.

MUTE DIALOGUE

QUESTION
How do you write dialogue for a character that is mute?

ANSWER
That depends on how that "dialogue" is communicated to the audience.

First of all, *signing* is not dialogue since words are not actually spoken. Of course, general audiences are not familiar with signing, so usually (in a film script) the mute person's meaning is communicated to the audience either orally or through subtitles. If the mute person speaks as she signs, then simply write the words she says as dialogue:

```
                    MUTE PERSON
                (while signing)
        Did you understand what I said?
```

If the mute person is a major character, then indicate once in the narrative description that the mute person signs whenever she talks; that way, you won't need to include a parenthetical for each block of dialogue.

If the dialogue is written in subtitles across the screen, then write out the dialogue as in the example above, except write the parenthetical as follows: "while signing; in subtitles." An alternative method is to indicate in narrative description that the mute person signs and that the dialogue appears in subtitles.

As always in spec writing, your goal is to be as clear and unobtrusive as you can.

EFFECTS THAT ARE SPECIAL

QUESTION
I have several scenes in my script that call for the use of special effects. It's not an "event" film, but a character piece that utilizes special effects for dramatic understanding.

My question is, how do you indicate the transition to the special effect? For example, do I write it as follows?

```
Steve takes a puff from the pipe.

FX. - WE SEE STEVE LEVITATE SLOWLY ABOVE
THE FLOOR, STILL IN HIS SQUATTED
POSITION.

STEVE'S POV - We then SEE the muted
COLORS of the room begin to BRIGHTEN
intensely.
```

Or do I simply write it as a normal scene description?

ANSWER
What you have written above is correct for a shooting script. In a spec script, avoid using technical language. When the script is converted into a shooting script, all the technical language will be added. Here's one way to revise this for a spec script.

```
Steve, sitting cross-legged on the floor,
takes a puff from the pipe. Slowly he
levitates.

He sees the muted colors of the room
brighten intensely.
```

That's it. You might consider breaking to a new paragraph for

"Slowly he levitates" to make that special effect stand out more, but no special language is required. Isn't that special?

I SPY

QUESTION
I want to write a movie scene where someone is under surveillance, but he doesn't know it. As we see him going up stairs into a public building, we hear (off screen) the sound of a 35 mm camera's shutter clicking. I would be interested in knowing how to write this in the proper format.

ANSWER
How about this?

```
EXT. PUBLIC BUILDING - DAY

James Connors hurries up the stairs.

An unseen person clicks the shutter of a
35 mm camera.  Clicks again.  And again
as James rushes into the building.
```

Of course, there are many ways to stage this scene and write the narrative. If you were writing a shooting script, you could use a POV (point-of-view) shot. If you feel so compelled, you could CAP the "clicks," since they are important sounds.

A SUPER JOB

QUESTION
Although I understand the use of SUPERs now, I'm unclear about how a spec script indicates that words are to appear on the screen...the way films will show a sentence to set

background history (or historical data) before the first scene. This would be like say, "California 1998" superimposed on the screen.

ANSWER
That's precisely what SUPER stands for—superimpose. When you write

```
SUPER: "California, 1998"
```

you are indicating that the words being quoted are to be superimposed over the image on the screen.

FOLLOW-UP QUESTION
What if it's more than one sentence? Also: If it appears at the beginning of the movie, does the writer simply type these sentences or *legends* out at the top of the script after "FADE IN:"?

ANSWER
First present an image, and then the superimposition. Here's an example that utilizes a longer "legend."

```
EXT. LOS ANGELES - DAY

The city sparkles in the sunlight.

SUPER: "Los Angeles, December 31, 1999.
It's an hour before midnight, an hour
before millions of computers pass into
oblivion...."
```

If you want to SUPER paragraphs, you may wish to consider using a SCROLL or ROLL-UP as in all of the STAR WARS episodes.

TREATMENT FORMAT

QUESTION
Is the normal 3-6 page selling treatment double-spaced?

ANSWER
Usually. Remember that a treatment is a written pitch—a marketing piece—and should include the character and her problem, the main turning points, and the emotional highlights. It should be written in narrative form with no or little dialogue.

LOST IN THE BOOKSTORE

QUESTION
I have a short scene in a bookstore. In the scene, a character goes into a restroom. Do I use a secondary heading? And how do I take the reader back into the bookstore—do I use the master scene heading again?

ANSWER
Just make the scene as clear as possible. First, establish the master scene with a master scene heading (slug line), and then use secondary headings to direct our eyes. Here's a possible list of headings in your scene, beginning with the master scene heading:

```
INT. BOOKSTORE - DAY

IN THE BATHROOM

BACK IN THE BOOKSTORE
```

...And so on, until you move to a location that requires a master scene heading.

QUOTES WITHIN DIALOGUE

QUESTION
Is it legal to use a quotation from Nietzsche in dialogue if the character speaking says, "Nietzsche says..."?

ANSWER
I am not qualified to give legal advice and nothing I write should be construed as such.

With that disclaimer out of the way, I can answer your question: Most likely yes. If it's just a line or two, you can quote most anyone. In one of my comedy *Kumquat*, my hero, a philosopher, has the worst day of his life. The punch line at the end of the scene goes like this.

                    PHILBERT
          So Kafka was right. Man is
          helpless to control his fate.

MINI-FLASHBACKS AND VOICE OVERS

QUESTION
How do you handle a quick memory hit? Let's say a man is telling a story to a friend about a friend getting killed by a train 30 years ago. Do I just write the image of a train killing David? [Apparently, David is the questioner's character who is killed; either that, or it's a secret message to me.] Do I need any caption such as a memory hit or quick flash?

ANSWER
A memory hit? I don't think that term has hit the mainstream formatting lexicon yet.

The standard response to questions of this type is this: Write

what we see. What does the audience see? If you actually
show the train, then that is a flashback and you will want to
indicate a flashback. You must label it as such so that we
clearly understand that it is a flashback.

If your character (let's call him Zep) speaks while we see the
flashback, then use the voice over (V.O.) device.

```
FLASHBACK - TRAIN TRACKS

David sees a train coming.  In a surreal
game of chicken, he places himself on the
tracks.

                    ZEP (V.O.)
          David always flirted with
          disaster...

With the train nearly upon him, David
tries to leap from the tracks, but his
shirt catches on a rail tie.

He glances up at the unforgiving mass of
steel.

                    ZEP (V.O.)
          ...Then one day, disaster
          responded.

The wheels of the train slice through his
body.
```

We can learn three lessons from the above example.

1. Notice that I avoided repeating in dialogue what we already
see visually. Whenever you use a voice over in situations like
this, let that voice over dialogue add something that the visual

does not already tell us. Don't just describe in your dialogue the action that you describe in your narrative.

2. Do not write something as general as "The train ran over him." Present us with concrete, visual images that we can respond to emotionally or intellectually.

3. Start a new paragraph when you switch to a new visual image. Generally, a paragraph of narrative description should present one visual image or one beat of action. (I hasten to add that that is a very general guideline.)

For more on flashback formatting, go on to the next question about dream sequences.

DREAM SEQUENCES

QUESTION
I'm writing a dream or a nightmare sequence as a reoccurring motif, but how do I inform the reader that it is a dream and not something else? Do I have to say something in the scene slug line like EXT. DREAM SEQUENCE, or do I just describe it in the action description? If so, what do I write? Is there a right or wrong way to do this?

ANSWER
As implied by my previous answer about flashbacks, you should clearly label anything that is not normal narrative action.

The exception comes when you want to hide that fact from the audience. In the situation you describe, I suspect that you want the reader to know that what he sees is a dream or dream sequence. (Incidentally, nightmares are dreams.) So let's approach your question from that angle.

First of all, you cannot write EXT. DREAM SEQUENCE because a dream sequence is not a location.

Second, make sure your heading (or slug line) is correctly labeled.

If the dream takes place in a single scene, just write:

```
EXT. CITY STREET - NIGHT - DREAM
```

or

```
EXT. CITY STREET - NIGHT (DREAM)
```

or

```
DREAM - A DIMLY LIT STREET
```

However, if this is a dream sequence that takes place over two scenes or more, write:

```
DREAM SEQUENCE

EXT. CITY STREET - NIGHT
```

Then write out the scenes until the dream ends, and then write:

```
END OF DREAM SEQUENCE
```

This same formatting style is used for flashbacks.

I hope these tips help you make your dreams come true.

A BLOCKBUSTER QUERY

QUESTION
I have just finished a script that could be the next blockbuster movie. Also, I have two other blockbuster scripts written. I'm thinking of querying all these scripts at the same time, indicating that all of them are blockbusters. What do you think?

ANSWER
The agent probably won't believe you. That's because many developing screenwriters make the same claim and then don't deliver. In fact, I've evaluated a number of "blockbusters" myself.

Additionally, your best strategy in a query is to *show* rather than *tell*. In other words, don't tell the agent you have three blockbusters; instead, pitch your biggest blockbuster in such a way that the agent can see that you have written a blockbuster. You may mention in your letter that you have two other scripts written.

Good luck and keep writing.

WORKING WITH DRILL INSTRUCTORS

QUESTION
Dr. Format, you have said to avoid exclamation points. I'm writing a spec script set in the military. There are scenes where drill instructors are barking orders at grunts. It seems to me that the script would lose its punch during scenes like that.

ANSWER
My advice is to *avoid* exclamation points, not eliminate them entirely. There are two main reasons to avoid them. First, you

don't want your dialogue looking like a garage sale ad. Second, you don't want to tell actors how to say their lines unless necessary. There is a line in the screenplay PLAY MISTY FOR ME that is followed by multiple exclamation points. However, in the movie, the actress says that line ever so softly, and it has a decidedly eerie and threatening effect.

Keep the next point in mind as well: If the context of the dialogue indicates that the actor would shout, then you don't need exclamation points because it's already obvious that he would shout. In your case, the military context is probably clear enough.   However, if you feel you are losing the "punch" of the scene, go ahead with the exclamation points, but consider using them only in moments where it's not otherwise obvious that the drill sergeant would be shouting.

Finally, using exclamation points or not using them is not going to make or break your script, unless your script starts looking like a want ad.

WORKING WITH PSYCHICS

QUESTION
My character is a psychic and he's giving another character an account of what he sees. If I'm trying to show the "account" visually with the character speaking, how do I write it?

ANSWER
Simply describe what we see on the screen. Write it like a regular scene with VOICE OVER (V.O.) dialogue. You will use VOICE OVER because the character speaking is not in the scene.

                    PSYCHIC (V.O.)
              You are coming into some money.

A homeless man holds out his hand and
receives a dollar from a passer-by.

WORKING WITH RABBIS

QUESTION
I am writing a funeral scene. The officiating rabbi is talking to
the mourners about the deceased. One of the characters
notices something happening on the cemetery road. I want to
write what the character sees, but at the same time, hear what
the officiating rabbi is saying. How do I do this?

ANSWER
What will the eventual movie audience see and hear? In this
case, they will see what is happening on the cemetery road
while they hear the words of the rabbi nearby. The rabbi is in
the scene, but not on screen, so his dialogue will be OFF
SCREEN (O.S.), as follows.

Sharon looks up the

CEMETERY ROAD

where three teenagers break into her car.

> RABBI (O.S.)
> The Lord giveth and the Lord
> taketh away.

WORKING WITH EMPATHS

QUESTION
Due to the science fiction nature of my script, some of my
characters are empaths or telepaths. How does one technically

say that the characters speak "empathically"? Do I write "empathically" as a parenthetical? Here's my example.

```
                    EMPATH
                (empathically)
      I am reading you, Chester.
```

ANSWER
Only spoken words can be written as dialogue. Dialogue is spoken speech. So you must find some other way. In STAR TREK, I have seen the empath simply state what she is *sensing* or *reading*. Thus, the audience knows what she is picking up.

Here is a question for *you*: If there is an actual telepathic communication, how will the *movie audience* know what is being communicated? In other words, what does the audience see and hear in the movie theater? Whatever it is, that is what you must describe in your screenplay. If the audience hears words (without anyone's lips moving), then clearly describe that and use a VOICE OVER for the words, although it's probably too hokey to use in a dramatic or serious work.

THE STORY'S THE THING

QUESTION
I have a scene in a large control room. The room is full of busy technicians conversing, including two main characters. Should I write the lines of everyone who speaks, including all of the background chatter and noise? It seems like a cop-out not including all the background chatter.

ANSWER
Unless the chatter is important to the essential story, why include it at all? Focus on the story.

QUESTION
I want to write a story about my wife who passed away. I want to show others what a caring person she was. I want to include a scene of her referring to her childhood when she wondered what she was going to be when she grew up. We won't see her talking; instead, we will see her as a child and also as what she wanted to become. How do I handle that?

ANSWER
There are two ways to handle this: 1) You present the visuals just as they will appear on the silver screen. Your wife's dialogue would be handled as a voice over. 2) If you decide to show her speaking, then you will cut to FLASHFORWARDS (if what we see is in the future) or FLASHBACKS (if what we see is in the past). A third choice would be to combine these two styles—sometimes we see her talking and sometimes she narrates (voice over).

A word of caution: This scene you refer to along with the screenplay will be a wonderful memory for you, but how will you make that memory come alive for an audience who never knew your wife and who have no emotional feeling for her when they walk into the theater?

Keep in mind that real life doesn't often translate naturally to dramatic structure. A true story almost always has to be restructured and changed, with time condensed and characters combined and events altered. And, of course, there must be a clear, compelling story with a beginning, middle, and end.

PHYSIOLOGY 101

QUESTION
When you are creating your characters for your script, do you have to determine all of the physiology? If I were to

determine that, then it would be hard for the director to find an actor for the role.

ANSWER
The physiology of your characters is seldom important to the screenplay for the reason you stated, but it should be important to you. You need to be able to visualize your character and have a definite "person" in mind when you write.

GOOD WILL TO ALL

QUESTION
Conventional wisdom suggests that there must be a clear goal and an antagonist, but I don't buy it. I've seen many movies where there appears to be neither a concrete goal nor an antagonist. Take GOOD WILL HUNTING. The movie seems completely driven by Will's need to love himself before he can be close to others. And the opposition is his own character flaws. Where's the goal?

ANSWER
That is a great question. In character-driven stories, the need almost always supersedes the goal. There are many movies where the goal is very thin or practically non-existent. (In STAND BY ME, the goal is to find the body.) In the case of GOODWILL HUNTING, notice the individual sequences. In those, you will see that Will often has an intention or desire; for example, he wants to put the arrogant college dude in his place and get Minnie Driver's phone number. That scene is driven by a goal that reveals something of his character.

Also, notice that there are at least two opposition characters. Robin Williams—and, to a lesser degree, Minnie Driver--oppose his goal/desire/intention to remain undiscovered and closed off from others and his own goodness. In addition,

Robin Williams is opposed by a colleague. And then, in individual scenes, you have the arrogant college dude, the university professor, and Will's best friend as opposition characters. So everyone has an intention, desire, or goal of some sort throughout the story, providing plenty of conflict. But at the core of the story is Will's need.

Your need (and goal) is to write a great story and gain the good will of an agent or producer.

WATCH YOUR FRENCH

QUESTION
In the screenplay I'm working on, I have a scene where the guests of a duchess are entertained by a tableaux vivant. How do I format the tableaux?

ANSWER
The first rule of formatting is to describe what we see. So what do we see in this tableaux? And where does it take place? Every scene has a location. The location is identified in the heading (slug line). I'm going to assume that we see this on a stage and that the duchess and her guests are in the audience.

```
INT. THEATER - NIGHT

The duchess and her guests gather in the
few luxury chairs that face a stage.

ON THE STAGE

the curtain rises to a tableaux vivant.
```

Now describe what the movie audience sees. What happens?

Occasionally, we may cut to the duchess who approves or disapproves with an applause or a gesture. This is essentially a play within a play. Just write what we see.

STUCK IN A MOVIE THEATER

QUESTION
I am trying to write a screenplay for which several scenes take place inside a movie theater. The action and dialogue that occur on the screen are integral to the story, but I'm not sure how to write the on-screen action to distinguish it from the action in the theater itself.

ANSWER
It sounds like you are going to have to cross-cut between the screen (ON THE SCREEN) and the theater (IN THE THEATER).

```
ON THE SCREEN

The Baywatch Kid draws his pistol.   Fires
twice.

IN THE THEATER

A disturbed young man stands and fires
back at the Baywatch Kid, only with real
bullets.
```

In addition, my responses to the tableaux vivant question above and the TV question on the next page will help you with this question because the three situations are related.

TELEVISION TALK

QUESTION
I'm writing a scene where people are watching a newscast on the television. We see the reporter on TV. How do I write what the reporter says?

In the next scene, we go to the White House where the reporter is reporting and we hear a continuation of his report.

ANSWER
In the first scene, do we see the reporter on TV or do we just hear him? If we just hear him, then it is VOICE OVER dialogue.

                    TV REPORTER (V.O.)
          I am standing in front of the
          White House...

If we see the reporter on TV as he speaks, then remove the VOICE OVER (V.O.).

Next, cut to the White House.

EXT. WHITE HOUSE - CONTINUOUS

The TV reporter continues. A huge crowd
observes.

                    TV REPORTER
          ...And, as you can see, it has
          been painted blue.

Incidentally, I used the ellipsis to show continuity in dialogue.

NO ONE IS COUNTING

QUESTION
How many lines per page are there in a screenplay?

ANSWER
About 53-54, but no one is counting unless the type looks cramped. Just set your margins correctly and you'll be in fine shape: 1.5 inches on the left, 1 inch on the right (you can stretch this to 1/2 inch if need be), and 1 inch on the top and bottom. See "Cheaters Never Prosper" on the next page.)

AS EASY AS CLASSICAL GREEK

QUESTION
My character is at a point of making a decision and will take an action either one way or the other. She recalls an event from the past, back to her, another event from the past, back to her, another event from the past, back to her, etc. Is this a series of shots? a montage? a flashback? Each event recalled is just a moment—it is clearly in her mind with the focus always on her.

I studied Classical Greek and it was easier than formatting.

ANSWER
There are several ways to handle this, whether in Greek or in English. Here are two.

1. Simply cross cut back and forth, from the present scene to a flashback, and so on. Each cut to the past is a flashback, regardless of how short that flashback is, but the focus will be on the decision. This style is similar to what M. Night Shyamalan did at the end of *The Sixth Sense* when Bruce Willis comes to his realization.

2. You could label the whole thing...

```
MONTAGE - SUSAN'S DECISION
```

...and then simply describe each shot that the audience will see. Every other shot will be a flashback and should be labeled as such.

In terms of content, I worry about this sequence just a little. What is this woman (we're calling her Susan) doing in the present as she moves forward to make her decision? I'm hoping she's physically moving towards some action and not in some kind of internal dialogue or chatting with a friend. Give the scene some movement and visual elements.

CHEATERS NEVER PROSPER

QUESTION
Can you cheat on the line spacing and add lines to a page?

ANSWER
Do not alter the spacing so that you can cram another line or two onto the page. Any professional reader will immediately recognize your deception, and he/she won't be happy about it. However, there are some adjustments you can make; see "Spaced Out" on page 120.

FOR WHOM THE BELL TOLLS

QUESTION
Which should be capitalized? "The BELL rang" or "The bell RANG"?

ANSWER
These days, neither. Just write, "The bell rang." If you wish, you may capitalize important sounds that you want to emphasize, in which case, it would be "The bell RANG."

THE WGA NOTICE

QUESTION
I find conflicting opinions as to whether or not it is proper to include a WGA notice and number on the title page of a script.

ANSWER
I suggest you type "Registered WGAw (or WGAe)" in the lower, left corner of the title page to show your script has been registered. However, there is no requirement to do that or to display your registration number. Make sure that you register your script with the WGA before you send it out to anyone.

ACTION STACKING

QUESTION
Lately I've been hearing about a popular way to write action called *action stacking*. I was wondering if you could give me an example of what this looks like. I don't think I have read a screenplay that shows this type of format.

ANSWER
Action stacking is a style of writing that literally stacks a series of short actions in a scene using single spacing. Here's an example.

```
EXT. BALLPARK - DAY
```

```
Duke sneers at the catcher.
He taps the bat twice on his cleats.
Spits a brown wad on home plate.
Allows himself a self-satisfied grin.
```

Notice that these are short sentences stacked one on top of the other; thus, *action stacking*. See my comments on pp. 71-72.

WRITING ACTION

QUESTION
On one hand, you say to dramatize important actions, while on the other hand, you say to "write lean." Can you provide an example of something that is both sparse and dramatic?

ACTION
I have seen many writers translate the word "lean" into "vague" or "no details." Actually, the opposite is true. "Writing lean" is choosing your details carefully and using specific, concrete words (especially verbs and nouns) to describe them. It's providing the reader with only what's necessary to *see* and *understand clearly* what's happening in the scene.

I would like to provide you with a "spec script" version of a brief excerpt from MISERY (© 1990 Castle Rock Entertainment, excerpted from *The Hollywood Scriptwriter*) by William Goldman. Annie is about to chop off Paul's foot with an axe.

```
PAUL

shrieks as there is a terrible thudding
sound -- and then his body jackknifes.
He is beyond agony as blood splashes over
his neck, his face, and
```

ANNIE

her face splashed with blood and

THE SHEET

turning red and

ANNIE

eyes dull, getting into position again.

                    ANNIE
          Once more and we're all done.

PAUL

as again there is the thudding sound, and
he's incoherent. Animal sounds come from
him as

ANNIE

takes a match, lights the propane torch
with the match, and there's a sound as
the yellow flame appears.

                    ANNIE
          No time to suture, got to
          cauterize.

She brings the flame closer. Paul
shrieks even louder.

                    ANNIE
          God, I love you....

Whew! Some novice writers would simply write:

```
She chops off his foot.  He screams
madly.  She lights the torch and
cauterizes the wound.
```

And there are others who might describe every detail over four pages. That, of course, would be *overwriting*.

I'd like to make one last comment about that last line of dialogue. Try to end your scenes with something that is strong, or something that moves us into the next scene or a future scene. In the above scene, we have a very strong punch line in Annie's declaration of "love."

WHAT'S IN A NAME?

QUESTION
If a character has a nickname throughout the movie (i.e., Killer), but his real name is Bob Franklin, do I call him Killer or Franklin or Bob where his name appears in the dialogue block [referring to the *character cue* or *character caption* in the dialogue block]?

ANSWER
It's your choice. Whichever you choose, it should be consistent throughout the entire script. When I say consistent, I mean a *consistent character cue*. In other words, whenever this character speaks, the character name you use (let's choose Franklin) should always be the same.

```
                FRANKLIN
          Be outa town by sunset or
          you're dead meat.
```

However, you can call him anything you want to in the narrative description and dialogue speeches. Just be consistent in the character cue. As a very general rule, by the way, call good guys by their first name and bad guys by their last name in the character cue.

FORMATTING QUERY LETTERS

QUESTION
I know that you recommend 12-point Courier (or New Courier) for screenplays, but what about query letters? Is Times New Roman or Arial cool, or should I stick to Courier? Any other formatting rules I should know? Also, what should be the word count for a query letter?

ANSWER
You have more latitude in a query letter, but keep in mind that your query letter is a business letter, although the actual content will reveal your true identity as a superb, creative writer. Fancy graphics are not necessary; after all, you are selling yourself as a writer, not as a graphic artist. But it's okay to format it to grab the reader's attention.

You may use Times New Roman or Arial, but don't use a script typeface or any typeface that might, in any way, be difficult to read. I favor a 12-point font. I also recommend standard block format, which means everything is brought to the left margin. Double space between paragraphs and don't indent. (But other formats are fine.)

As to word count, I don't count words. I shoot for three "brief" paragraphs, maybe four. However, the letter needs to be long enough to convince the reader to call you, but short enough to lure someone into reading it. Big blocks of black ink won't do that.

HOW HIGH IS HIGH?

QUESTION
Does the notion of "high concept" apply to family movies as well? When I think of *Otis and Milo* and *Homeward Bound*, I see similar concepts of animals trying to get home. If these films were still in the scripting stage, I wouldn't think they were high concept. Do you think they are?

ANSWER
Both of these movies have a concept—in other words, they can be conceptualized. Whether that concept is "high" or not is in the mind of the producer. One person might say "yes" for his particular market, while another may say "no" for her market.

The point is you need to be able to conceptualize your story. What is the concept? What is the story in 25 words or less? What is it about your story that will make your reader say "Now that's a movie"? A particularly strong rendition of the concept is called "high concept" because it makes the reader/listener feel "high"—"Ah, this is a movie I can sell to my market."

LOG LINES

QUESTION
What makes a good log line?

ANSWER
A book could be written on this (and has by Michael Hauge), and the above explanation on "high concept" should be of some value to you. Here are additional ideas. A good logline is about a character with a problem that grabs the reader and says, "I am a movie."

A good logline is just that—one line, one sentence. A good logline can be a premise question (What if the president were kidnapped?) or a statement around a big event (When a child psychiatrist is shot by a patient, he redeems himself by helping a child who sees ghosts overcome his fear of them). In virtually all cases, a logline cannot sell a script, but a good logline can position the movie in the reader's mind and make him or her want to read more.

SAY IT IN ENGLISH

QUESTION
Is "sotto voce" or simply "sotto" still used in parentheticals these days?

ANSWER
There's no need to use Latin unless you are a priest or a music composer. Besides, you want to avoid soliloquies in spec scripts these days. If you must have a character say something to himself that the other characters do not hear, just use the term "aside" or "to self" or don't use a parenthetical at all.

AN UN*BEAT*ING STRATEGY

QUESTION
What thoughts do you have on the use of the term "beat" in dialogue? According to Denny Martin Flinn, we should not use the term. He says to write "pause" or to detail the intended beat with a specific action.

ANSWER
I am in with Flinn. The term "beat" is a theatrical term and, although you see it in many shooting scripts and in Joe Ezsterhaus's spec scripts, you can certainly find something

more exciting than "beat." After all, you *are* a creative writer. Which of the following three examples creates more interest?

                    JANE
        Ed Darling, I want you to
        know...
                (beat)
        ...how much I love you.

                    JANE
        Ed Darling, I want you to
        know...
                (eyes mist up)
        ...how much I love you.

                    JANE
        Ed Darling, I want you to
        know...
                (suddenly sneezing
                all over Ed)
        ...how much I love you.

None of the three examples will win any prizes, but certainly the first is the boring one. The second is dramatic. The third is funny (or disgusting). Here is the point. The word "beat" is the most colorless, lifeless term you can use to indicate a pause. Instead, use specific words that add to the story or help characterize your character.

LATE ARRIVAL

QUESTION
If I were to introduce a character first through off-screen dialogue, what would I call him/her? Would you still use his/her name, even though he/she has not yet been introduced to the reader?

ANSWER
Try to introduce the character before she speaks. If you can't do that, then use her name, or use the cue FEMALE VOICE (assuming the character is a woman); and then, once we see her and you introduce her, start using her name as your character cue. Here's a quick example.

```
                FEMALE VOICE
       I want to tell you....

Ed parts the curtain and sees JANE, a
twenty-something bombshell with hair
tumbling everywhere.

                JANE
       ...how much I love you.
```

INSERTING THE GUN

QUESTION
How many INSERTS are allowed in a spec script?

ANSWER
Limit your use of INSERT. In many cases, you may not need to use it at all. For example, if you want to emphasize the fact that there is a gun lying on the coffee table, simply write:

```
A gun lies on the coffee table.
```

THE WRITER AS DIRECTOR

QUESTION
We know that long before a script becomes a movie it is first a reading experience, and that we should avoid camera

directions because that's the director's job. But there is a definite feel I wish to communicate in my first page. Here it is.

```
EXT. HIGHWAY 27 - DAY - AERIAL VIEW

WE SEE the lush Florida countryside until
we FIND our subject, a dark blue van.

SLOW ZOOM IN ON VAN

VIEW ON VAN - MOVING

Two characters shout at each other while
the CAMERA MOVES beside the van until we
see the child/protagonist looking out the
window at us.

INT. VAN

Everyone is quiet.
```

ANSWER
I would not call the above a riveting "reading experience." Notice in the above example that the focus is on *how* the story is told, not on the story itself. What is going on in the car? We don't know. Who are the characters? Why is the child looking out the window? What is his or her facial expression? Is the child a boy or a girl? We don't know because you are too involved *directing* your movie.

How can you improve this without sacrificing much in terms of the "feel" that you want to communicate? The revision that follows is not a masterpiece, but I hope you find it a better read than the original.

```
EXT. FLORIDA - DAY
```

From the Atlantic shore, the lush
countryside extends for miles westward.

Below, a black two-lane highway meanders
through the spring growth.

A rusted-out van scoots down the highway.

EXT./INT. VAN - SAME

The van rumbles along. Inside, two
twenty-something parents, BUSTER and
CAROL shout at each other, although their
words cannot be heard.

Buster shoots an angry look to the back
where LISA, age 6, leans away from him
and stares out the window at the
beautiful trees and shrubs whizzing by.

AT THE WINDOW

The child's are sad. She sits
motionless, looking trapped. One little
hand presses against the window.

BACK IN THE VAN

The parents are silent now -- gathering
steam before their next eruption.

In the revision, I have *suggested* almost everything you
wanted, but my focus is on the story and the characters, not on
fancy-dancy ways to tell the story.

In addition, I also *imply* a POV shot of the child staring at the
trees and shrubs. If desired, I could even describe the

reflection of trees on the window glass (without using technical terms).

I also direct the camera (without using a camera direction) to a CLOSE UP of the child at the window. And I do that for a story reason. I want the reader to know that the child is the most important character in the scene, and that maybe she is the central character or protagonist; and I want the reader (and the movie audience) to emotionally identify with the child's situation.

I end the scene with a promise of things to come. I am trying to create some interest in what happens next while revealing the emotions of the parents.

In summary, my advice is to focus on story and character; and, while you are at it, use clear, specific language.

SILENCE IS GOLDEN

QUESTION
What does MOS mean?

ANSWER
It means without sound. The reason it is MOS instead of WOS is because it originates with German director Eric von Stroheim, who would say, "Ve'll shoot dis mid out sound."

With MOS, we see the characters' lips moving, but we don't hear their voices or the sounds around them. As an example, the fourth paragraph on page 60 could be written as follows:

```
The van rumbles along.  Inside, two
twenty-something parents, BUSTER and
CAROL shout at each other MOS.
```

MAKING SCENES

QUESTION
I am not clear on the use of DAY. It seems redundant to keep writing DAY in scene after scene that takes place within a single sequence. For example, if I am outside a warehouse and then move inside the warehouse, do I have to use DAY in both cases, as follows?

```
EXT. WAREHOUSE - DAY

INT. WAREHOUSE - DAY
```

ANSWER
First, let's discuss the fundamentals, then apply them.

Every *master scene* consists of three elements: 1) camera placement (EXT or INT), 2) location, and 3) time (usually DAY or NIGHT). Technically, when any one of the three elements changes, the scene changes. That's why *master scene headings* have three parts, one for each of the three elements that comprise a scene.

Thus, when you move the camera inside the warehouse, you create a new scene that requires a new scene heading (slug line). That means that your two master scene headings above are correct.

If you feel that the repetition of DAY is redundant, you can apply certain alternatives as long as the three elements of the scene are clear to the reader.

If one scene follows the other scene in one continuous line of action without any jumps in time, you can write CONTINUOUS or SAME. Here's an example.

```
EXT. WAREHOUSE - DAY

Jake unlocks the warehouse door and
pushes the door open.

INT. WAREHOUSE - CONTINUOUS

Jake steps into the warehouse.
```

If that exterior scene is only there to establish Jake's presence and introduce the scene inside the warehouse, then you can use this alternative.

```
EXT./INT. WAREHOUSE - CONTINUOUS

Jake unlocks the warehouse door and steps
in.
```

That device is often used in car scene conversations. It gives the director the choice to place the camera inside the car or outside the car or both.

Occasionally, you can get away with omitting DAY, as follows.

```
EXT. WAREHOUSE - DAY

Jake unlocks the warehouse door and
pushes the door open.

INT. WAREHOUSE

Jake steps into the warehouse.
```

Only do that when the time (DAY or NIGHT) is absolutely clear to the reader, as in the example above. Sometimes writers get fancy or clever in their headings, only to confuse the reader.   Clarity is one of the prime keys to great spec writing.

MASTERING SCENES

QUESTION
I've noticed that some screenplays use the complete slug line INT. BEDROOM - NIGHT [with all three scene elements included] while others use IN THE BEDROOM. Which is correct, or is it writer's choice?

ANSWER
Please note my use of the term *master scene heading* in my previous answer. A master scene heading is a heading (slug line) for a *master scene*. That master scene may (or may not) contain more than one *mini scene* or *beat of action*. This is best illustrated through an example.

In the example below, I first write the master scene heading, specifying the camera placement, the *primary location*, and the time of day. Within this primary location, there will be other *secondary locations* that are part of the primary location. I will not need a full master scene heading for those secondary locations. Instead, I will use *secondary headings*. Ready?

```
INT. MILLIE'S HOUSE - NIGHT

Millie steps in and shuts the door.  In a
flash, she races up the stairs and into

THE LONG HALL

where she suddenly slows her pace,
noticing a dim yellow light spilling
under the bedroom door.
```

```
IN THE BEDROOM

Bart waits nervously, clenching his .38
special in his hand.

IN THE HALL

Millie stares at the doorknob for a slow
moment -- calculating -- then quietly
opens the door.
```

Of course, the above master scene (containing all the little mini-scenes) will continue until we change the camera placement, the primary location, or the time of day. At that point, we will begin a new master scene with a new master scene heading.

Many writers triple space before master scene headings (rather than double space), and that's fine. But you should not triple space before or after secondary scene headings.

SLUG LINES

QUESTION
Why do you use the terms *master scene heading* and *secondary scene heading* instead of *slug line* like everyone else.

ANSWER
I get asked that all the time. The term *slug line* is actually a journalistic term. In screenwriting, there are two kinds of headings that *head* scenes, and I want to be clear to my readers as to which is which. My great desire is that your scenes be masterful.

SUBLIMINAL SCRIPTWRITING

QUESTION
There is a sequence in my screenplay where there are flashes
of images, like TOM IN A CHAIR, TOM IN MOTEL
ROOM, TOM DEAD IN THE ALLEY—quick flashes in an
almost subliminal fashion. How would I format this?

ANSWER
The "flashes" are either subliminal or they are not. Just write
what we see. There are many ways to handle this. Consider
using the SERIES OF SHOTS if the flashes tell a little story;
in other words, if they outline a narrative. Use the
MONTAGE if these flashes revolve around a concept, such as
passage of time.

```
SERIES OF SHOTS - TOM'S DEATH

A) Tom sits in a chair -- silent.

B) Tom paces in a motel room, then
glances towards the door.

C) Tom lies dead in an alley.
```

If these must be quick flashes to get the right effect, then use
the following:

```
SERIES OF QUICK FLASHES

-- Tom sits in a chair.

-- Tom paces in a motel room.

-- Tom lies dead in an alley.
```

SCHOOL DAYS

QUESTION
Within my script, the main character walks to and from school several times. I've established him leaving his house (EXT. JOSH'S HOUSE) and arriving at school (EXT. LINCOLN HIGH SCHOOL). What about the journey between the two locations? Generally, nothing happens along the way (no actions or dialogue). How do I write this? Do I refer to it as "EXT. ROUTE TO SCHOOL"? Or do I mention it at all?

ANSWER
If you have read my column with any regularity, you know that the answer to half the questions I receive is "Write what we see." And that's the case here. Apparently, we don't see the route between home and school, so write something like this.

```
EXT. JOSH'S HOUSE - DAY

Josh exits the house throwing on his
backpack jammed with books. He rushes
through the front yard to the road.

EXT. LINCOLN HIGH SCHOOL - LATER

Josh arrives on the school grounds.
```

NOISES OFF

QUESTION
I noticed in a produced spec script that the writer only capitalized sounds that really exploded with description. For example: Tires CRACKLED across the broken glass. In other cases, the writer did not capitalize sounds at all. Is this something new? Or is it all discretionary?

ANSWER

Yes and yes. The current trend is towards *not* placing sounds in all-CAPS. However, many writers still use all-CAPS for very important sounds. It's at your discretion, but there is no longer any "requirement" to capitalize sounds in a spec script. I hasten to add that every agent and producer has his or her own preferences, but the above is generally true.

LET'S ESTABLISH ONE THING

QUESTION

I have searched all the books and cannot seem to find the right camera angle/direction for this shot. I have an establishing shot focusing on a parade. The camera must rise above the parade to an aerial shot of the city. The camera will move over the city and lower to the main location in the film. The film begins in the present and immediately flashes back to 1974. The aerial shot is used as a time transition. What do you suggest?

ANSWER

The reason you are having difficulty finding this camera direction is because it is not used in spec scripts. I assume you are writing a script on spec and that you have not been paid to write it. If so, you want to *avoid* camera angles and editing directions. That doesn't mean you can't direct the camera *without* camera directions. If you absolutely must have this shot, just write it out in narrative description.

```
We move up from the parade and over the
city until we descend into Central Park.
```

Just write it as simply as that. The reason most producers and agents react negatively to camera directions is because your job is to write the story, not direct the movie.

THE FIRST CUT IS THE DEEPEST

QUESTION
Do you really believe that using "cut to" in your spec scripts really hurts your chance of being taken seriously? And if so, why do I see CUT TO throughout every script I read? For example, look at THE CONVERSATION by Coppola.

ANSWER
Let's take the second question first. Virtually every script available for purchase is a *shooting script*, but you are writing a *spec script*. Don't assume spec style is the same as shooting style (which is filled with technical directions). It is extremely difficult to get your hands on a sold spec script—they are rare. So I'm guessing that the scripts you are referring to are shooting scripts.

Also, writers who also direct or produce don't have to please anyone but themselves. You ought to see a Woody Allen script—it's not even close to correct format.

Now, the first question. Obviously, if your script is wonderful, but contains some CUT TOs, it is not going to be rejected. But readers, agents, and producers who read dozens of scripts a week will glance through a script (before they begin reading it) to see if it is in spec format. The little things add up to make a good or bad first impression. Just one or two things are not going to make a difference. But if you know better, why push it? Use editing directions sparingly.

As an additional comment, not every Hollywood type reacts the same way. There are probably many who are not that focused on form and could care less. But generally, people look at scripts the same way you and I look at the want ads--they're seeing how many they can eliminate or screen out immediately.

DO YOU HEAR WHAT I HEAR?

QUESTION
If a hearing-impaired character has dialogue in the form of sign language, what is the proper format for writing it?

ANSWER
If the character uses sign language, then that is action and not dialogue. The question is how do you convey the *meaning* of that sign language to the audience? Well, it's hard to imagine subtitles for sign language, except maybe in a comedy. The only remaining option is to have a character interpret that sign language for another character in the scene, and that interpretation would be dialogue.

TO MONTAGE OR NOT TO MONTAGE

QUESTION
According to a recent article, alphabetically listing montage shots has become passe in spec scripts. If so, what is the correct format?

ANSWER
First, it never was correct format to alphabetically list MONTAGE shots. That is only done with the SERIES OF SHOTS device. (As a reminder, use the MONTAGE to communicate a concept, such as passage of time, and use the SERIES OF SHOTS for a narrative. Also, keep in mind that these two devices are often used interchangeably, though the MONTAGE format is most often used by writers.)

Here's what a MONTAGE should look like.

```
MONTAGE - DELBERT AND EDITH FALL IN LOVE
```

-- They share lunch at the park. Delbert
gets mayo on his face. Edith laughs.

-- Delbert jumps up and shrieks when the
ants get him. Edith laughs.

-- They row a boat across a lake.
Delbert stands to sing and falls into the
lake. Edith laughs.

-- They change the oil of Delbert's rusty
Ford Farlane. Delbert paints his face
with oil -- it's war paint -- and dances
and whoops around the car. Edith laughs.

STACKING ACTIONS

QUESTION
Can I "action stack" for selected scenes and use a [traditional] narrative style for others, or do I have to be consistent throughout my screenplay?

ANSWER
You can combine styles, but don't use one style (action stacking, for example) just once in a screenplay.

Action stacking is...well..."stacking" short sentences that describe action without double spacing between those sentences. Here's an example.

Bart spins around.
A truck speeds towards him.
Bart dives for the gutter.
Looks up a pair of legs.
The leggy woman looks down.
She has a gun.

Personally, I'm not a big fan of action stacking and I don't see it a lot, but it's perfectly legal. However, if you use it, show some consistency of writing style throughout your screenplay.

SPACING OUT

QUESTION
Regarding triple spacing prior to new master scenes, if I have a continuous sequence that involves different locations, should I still triple space for new scenes that are in that sequence?

ANSWER
You do not need to triple space at all. It is optional. Some people like to triple space before master scenes, and that's okay, but not required.

Again, to explain, a *master scene* takes place in a master location. For example, perhaps you open a scene with INT. SMITH HOUSE - DAY. If you then cut to the BEDROOM in that house, and then the DEN, and then the WINE CELLAR, those locations are all part of the larger location (the house), so we are still within the same master scene.

As you know, you normally double space between scenes. But, as an option, you can triple space before master scene headings, but not before scene headings within a master scene.

FOLLOW-UP QUESTION
Should I triple space if I use a new master scene heading to establish a second location for an intercut telephone conversation?

ANSWER
I suggest that you double space to maintain a sense of continuity.

A SUPER QUOTE

QUESTION
How does one present a quote or an introductory piece of text at the very beginning of the film? A SUPER does not seem quite right, since the text is over a black screen.

ANSWER
Just SUPER (superimpose) the quote, text, prologue, or ROLL-UP over the black screen. And after typing

SUPER:

double space, and indent ten spaces for the quote—just as you would for dialogue. See page 151 for an example.

POTTY TALK

QUESTION
Is profanity and the f-word allowable in spec script dialogue, or is that something for the actors to add?

ANSWER
You want slightly less profanity and vulgarity in the screenplay than you would find in the eventual movie. I have heard this advice from many agents and producers.

Of course, virtually everything is "allowable" in a screenplay, including profanity. It all depends on the market you are writing for, so my advice is to look carefully at the market you are writing for.

GETTING ANIMATED

QUESTION
I am working on a script for a film that would contain several short animated segments. How should these be worked into the script? Is there a standard format for this?

ANSWER
Handle it just the way you'd handle a DREAM or FLASHBACK or MONTAGE that you need to work into the script. Here's one possible way:

```
ANIMATION -- SILLY BILLY MEETS THE MONKEY
MAN
```

And then describe your scene or sequence of shots, just as you would with a MONTAGE or DREAM SEQUENCE.

We often forget that there are basic principles behind formatting. These aren't just a bunch of arbitrary rules. So don't be afraid to extrapolate from some known principle if you come up with a new screenwriting situation. What if the above were a dream sequence? Handle it like this.

```
DREAM -- SILLY BILLY MEETS THE MONKEY MAN
```

or

```
EXT. AMAZON JUNGLE - DREAM

Silly Billy and his friends hike the
jungle trail.  Suddenly, the Monkey Man
drops out of a tree.
```

...And so on.

What if you have an animated dream? Just call it that, an

ANIMATED DREAM.

If you have a particularly long FLASHBACK, DREAM, MONTAGE, SERIES OF SHOTS, or ANIMATED SEQUENCE—just label it. For example:

DREAM SEQUENCE

And then write out all of the scenes in the sequence, just as you would normally write scenes, and then end the sequence with this:

END OF DREAM SEQUENCE

Or, you could label each scene with an appropriate suffix.

EXT. JUNGLE - DAY - DREAM SEQUENCE

EXT. MOUNTAIN TRAIL - CONTINUOUS - DREAM SEQUENCE

Just apply fundamental formatting principles and strive for clarity. As screenwriters, we must understand formatting to fully understand spec writing. This is something I really get animated about.

THIS IS MY CHARACTER

QUESTION
How detailed should I be with the appearance of a new character? Do I describe only those with speaking parts? Do I describe past circumstances, such as "Josh's father left when Josh was just a baby," or "Kelly's sister Sharon is far more outgoing and, as a newspaper editor, loves to dig for the dirt."

ANSWER
First, let's set up the guidelines.

Guideline #1: You can only describe what we (the audience; the reader) actually see and actually hear in narrative description. Occasionally, you can cheat a little in character descriptions, but don't go so far as to tell us someone's history as a character introduction. Don't write something like *Jenny used to be a cocktail waitress and had an affair with Jane's husband just a year ago, although Jane doesn't know it yet.* You cannot do that because it cannot appear on the silver screen, but you can say that Mark is Jenny's wife or that Jane is Jenny's sister—you can probably get away with that.

Guideline #2: With character descriptions, focus on *character* and make the description visual in some way. My favorite example is from a client: *She wears clothes that are too young for her, but gets away with it.* Do you see that the description is visual, but that it also says something about her *character*? That's what you want to strive for.

Okay, now let's answer your questions above.

I'll answer the second question first. Characters without speaking parts do not necessarily need an introduction. However, you want every character to be clearly visualized by the reader.

For minor characters, you can do that with just a few words that makes the reader see them. For example, "He's proud of his pony tail" (it's visual and says something about his character) or "wearing a Metallica tee-shirt" (it's visual and says something about his character).

For characters with speaking parts, it is even more important to give them some handle that the reader can grab them with. Here's a description of a character from SCREAM:

BILLY LOOMIS, a strapping boy of
seventeen. A star quarterback/class
president type of guy. He sports a smile
that could last for days.

Now, the writer doesn't say that Billy is class president or star quarterback, just that he is that type of guy. The description is visual and says something about his character.

Also, note that there is no driver's license description of Billy Loomis. The writer doesn't mention height, weight, eye color, or hair color. Why? Because it's not important to the story. Only mention those physical details when it is crucial to the story. (For example, it is important that Elle is a blonde in *Legally Blonde*.) For the most part, focus on character.

WHO'S ON FIRST?

QUESTION
In the screenplay I am working on, I have a sequence where the camera is the character's eye. During this sequence, the story is told in first person. I would be interested in knowing how to insert this sequence into a screenplay written in third person without [using] technical intrusions.

ANSWER
When you say the "story is told in first person," I assume you mean that the character (whose eye is the camera) talks to or describes what he/she is sees. Thus, that character's *viewpoint* dominates in that scene. However, the narrative description would still be written in third person.

Narrative description is always written in third person, present tense language. (First person would involve the use of the pronouns "I" or "me." Second person would use "you." And third person would use "he," "she," "they," and so on.) The fact that the eye is the camera changes nothing in terms of how you write description and dialogue.

That leaves the issue of communicating to the reader that the "camera is the character's eye." I assume that you mean that the camera takes the point-of-view of the character—what he/she sees, we see. You are right to want to write this without the camera directions, if possible. In cases like this, we are all tempted to write something like the following:

```
POV JANE -- A man walks towards her.
```

You can (and should) write the same thing without the camera direction, as follows:

```
Jane sees a man walk towards her.
```

(Incidentally, both examples are written in third person, present tense.)

Of course, if everything in the entire scene is seen from Jane's point-of-view, you could simply begin the scene with a note.

```
(NOTE:  Everything we see in this scene
is from Jane's point-of-view, as if her
eye is the camera.)
```

Yes, I realize that such a note is an intrusion on the story, but a rare intrusion is permissible if it clearly explains something that is important to the story.

Of course, that begs the question, *how important is this POV stuff to the story?* If you are just dressing up the scene for effect, you might be making a mistake. Your job is to tell the story in clear, visual terms, not direct the movie.

THE LITTLEST ORPHAN

QUESTION
I have been taught to never leave a slug line [heading] or character cue as an "orphan"; that is, never leave any of these as the last item on the bottom of the page. Does this also apply to "direction" [parentheticals; actor's instructions]?

ANSWER
You are correct all the way around. Do not end a page on a slug line, character cue, or parenthetical. Just move those to the top of the next page, if at all possible.

S-S-STUTTERING AND DIALECTIN'

QUESTION
I am writing a screenplay where the main character stutters almost all the time. How should I indicate that in the dialogue? I find it annoying to indicate it in parenthesis before every line of dialogue, so I came up with something like the following:

```
                    JOHN
          W-what?   I-I d-don't
          understand.
```

Do you have any suggestions?

ANSWER
Just show a flavor of stuttering; that is, occasional stuttering to remind us that this character stutters. Don't overdo it or, as you rightly said, the reader will be annoyed. Also, when you first introduce the character, indicate that he/she stutters.

The same holds true for accents and dialects—just give the

reader a flavor.   Don't adjust the spelling of every word to show precisely how each and every word would be pronounced in a certain dialect or with a certain accent.   It will be too difficult to read.

HOW LONG IS TOO LONG?

QUESTION
How long should a [spec] screenplay be?

ANSWER
About 100-110 pages, but certainly not more than 120 pages. Ideally, a comedy will come in at about 100 pages and a drama or action story at 105-110.   The minimum is 90.   These are just guidelines, not hard-fast rules.   An MOW (movie-of-the-week script) should come in at around 100-105 pages.

You may wonder why the 120-page limit when you've seen produced screenplays that are much longer than that.   In virtually every case, those long screenplays were developed within the system; they were not spec screenplays.

The central theme that runs through this issue's column is to make your spec screenplay an "easy but fascinating read."

LOOK WHO'S TALKING

QUESTION
What is the proper format to use for an animal that makes animal sounds, but who also talks?

For example: A dog barks, then in a human voice says, "Hey, cut that out!"

ANSWER
Animal sounds should be written as narrative description. That's because only words are considered to be dialogue. Thus, you would write your example as follows.

Sparky barks, then speaks in English.

                    SPARKY
           Hey, cut that out!

I SCREAM, YOU SCREAM

QUESTION
How does one write non-conversational vocal sounds, like screams? Are they written as action [narrative description]? Or are they placed under a character's name [as in the example below]?

                    LORI
              (screams)

ANSWER
Write screams and human sounds (other than speech) as narrative description. The following is correct.

Lori screams.

Notice that I did not write the sound (screams) in all-CAPS. You may CAP important sounds if you wish, but it is no longer necessary in spec writing.

PARENTHETICAL ACTION

QUESTION
I have been told that I cannot end a dialogue block with an action as shown below. Is that true?

```
              GERTIE
     I'm going to make you hurt.
           (smiling with
           devilish delight)
```

ANSWER
You have been told correctly. You should not end a dialogue block with an action. You can handle this situation in one of two ways.

```
              GERTIE
           (smiling with
           devilish delight)
     I'm going to make you hurt.
```

Or...

```
              GERTIE
     I'm going to make you hurt.

She smiles with devilish delight.
```

DIALOGUE IS DIALOGUE

QUESTION
I have a scene where a character discovers a journal and reads an entry from it. Since it's not really up to me whether the character reads the entry aloud or if the actual entry is displayed on screen, how should I format this in the script?

ANSWER

Before I answer the question, let me make two points. First, don't be ambiguous in a screenplay. Write what we see and hear. Either the character reads the journal out loud or the audience reads it silently—you decide in the screenplay. Yes, the director may change what you wrote later, but at least give her a vision of what *you* see.

Second, only dialogue is dialogue. You can only write in dialogue words that are spoken.

Now, in answer to your question, I see two ways to approach this formatting problem.

1. If the journal entry is very short, you might consider allowing the audience to read it. Use the INSERT for this.

```
INSERT - NATASHA'S JOURNAL, which reads:

          "I love Boris, but I plan to
          leave him for Fearless Leader."
```

2. If the journal entry is longer, then perhaps your character can read it to the audience.

```
Boris tiptoes into Natasha's room, spots
her journal, and turns to the last page.
His eyes soften.

                    NATASHA (V.O.)
          I love Boris, but his silly
          mustache tickles me.  I plan to
          leave him for Fearless Leader.
```

As you can see, all of this month's questions have to do with writing dialogue and writing action that is connected with dialogue. I hope your dialogue brings you a lot of action.

THE DREADED WRYLIES

QUESTION
Suppose my character joins the foreign legion and speaks in French, do I use the dreaded wrylies to explain that he is speaking in French? Or do I write the dialogue in French? Or should I use subtitles?

ANSWER
I've had legions of questions about foreign languages, so I am using the above as representative of them all. Even though I have addressed this issue briefly in a previous column, the time has come for a full treatise. First, let me explain the question.

The writer refers to "dreaded wrylies." Wrylies are the parentheticals that sometimes appear before dialogue speeches. The term developed because so many novice writers used the term "wryly" to describe their characters' dialogue. For example:

                          SAM
                    (wryly)
              And when you lay down tonight,
              remember to fall asleep.

And so the term *wryly* was born. The reason they are "dreaded" is because writers are encouraged to use them sparingly. Only use a *wryly* when the subtext of the dialogue is not otherwise clear. You may also use them to describe small actions that can be described in two or three words, such as *lighting his cigar* or *smiling wistfully*.

Using foreign languages
In working with other languages, realize there is one general rule: write your script in the language of the eventual reader so

that he/she knows what is going on. In other words, avoid writing dialogue in a foreign language.

If a character speaks in French, do not write out the dialogue in French unless the eventual reader is French, or in the extremely rare case that the meaning of the words don't matter. Simply write the lines as follows:

```
                  JEAN-MARC
              (in French)
       Come with me to the Casbah.
```

Now the observant reader is likely to say, "But Dave, the word 'Casbah' is a French word." Yes, however it's also an English word with French and African roots, but the observant reader brings up a good point.

Instead of having your character speak in French, consider sprinkling his/her dialogue with French words to give us the flavor of French. Then everyone knows what is being said.

Now, suppose your character absolutely, positively must speak in a foreign language. Your desire is for something realistic, such as the Italian spoken in *The Godfather*. You have five options, depending on your specific purpose.

1. If it doesn't matter whether the audience understands the meaning of the foreign words, or if you believe the audience will be able to figure out the meaning of the words by their context, then just write them in the foreign language. For example:

```
Tarzan shouts at the charging elephant.

                  TARZAN
          On-gow-ah!
```

```
The elephant turns and stampedes in the
opposite direction.
```

Or write the words in English using a *wryly* to indicate what language the words will be spoken in, as follows:

```
                PIERRE-LUC
             (in French)
      Imbecile.  Idiot.  Retard.
```

2. If the characters speak in French throughout an entire scene, then make a clear statement in the narrative description that all the dialogue in the scene will be spoken in French; then, write the dialogue out in English so that the reader can understand it.

...But this begs the question: How will the ***audience*** know what is being said? They won't unless they are French. For that reason, this is seldom a viable option. If your character must speak in French and it's also important that the audience understand what is being said, then the solution is subtitles.

Subtitles
3. If you write a long scene where French (or other language) is spoken and if you want English subtitles to appear on the movie screen while the character speaks in French, then include a special note in the narrative description, as follows:

```
NOTE: The dialogue in this scene is
spoken in French with English subtitles.
```

Then, simply write the dialogue out in English. After the scene ends, write:

```
END OF SUBTITLES
```

4. Another option for using subtitles is to use our friend, the "dreaded wryly."

```
                    MICHELLE
              (in French, with
              subtitles)
        I spit on your name.  I spit
        on your mother's grave.  I
        spit on your column.

The spittle flies.
```

5. There is one other option for using subtitles. Use this device only if the sound of the words in the foreign language is important; for example, in the case of this space visitor's language, the words have a humorous quality.

```
        ALIEN                    SUBTITLES
   Zoo-BEE, Woo-BEE.       You're cute.
```

My final advice is to choose English whenever possible and give us a flavor of the foreign language by including a few foreign words and/or flavor of a foreign accent. So until my next column, I bid you *adieu*.

SIMULTANEOUS DIALOGUE

QUESTION
When two characters say the same line at the same time, how do you format that?

ANSWER
Here's the first of four ways to present two people speaking at the same time.

```
                    SAM AND JO
          Huh, what?
```

Or you can add a parenthetical to make it absolutely clear.

```
                    SAM AND JO
               (together)
          Huh, what?
```

Or replace the word "together" with "simultaneously."

Here's a third example that you can use when the two characters say the same thing at about the same time or when they say *different* things at about the same time.

```
                    SAM
          Huh, what?


                    JO
               (overlapping)
          Huh, what?
```

And finally...

```
          SAM                    JO
     Huh, what?            Huh, what?
```

LOCATING THE LOCATION

QUESTION
If, for dramatic purposes, you cut to the next scene by using a stark image—BLOODY FINGERS, for example—would you do something like this for the slug line: INT. BARN BLOODY FINGERS – NIGHT?   Or would you just write BLOODY FINGERS, and then pull back and describe the situation?

ANSWER
Since BLOODY FINGERS is not a location, it would not
appear in the slug line. Write it as follows:

```
INT. BARN - NIGHT

Bloody fingers tremble.  They reach for
the barn door.
```

In the above description, I focus the reader's attention on the
fingers first, and then on the action and surroundings. That
implies that we open the scene with a CLOSE UP on the
bloody fingers, and then the camera PULLS BACK (or
PANS) so that we see the barn door (and barn interior). Thus,
we present a clear, visual image to the reader without using
camera directions.

ACTION SHOULD COMMENT
ON CHARACTER

QUESTION
I'm presently writing a script that involves a lot of comings
and goings of characters. Thus, I find myself often using the
same exit and enter lines: Charlie enters or Charlie leaves.
Would this method be too repetitious?

ANSWER
Yes. Be more specific and concrete than "Charlie enters" and
"Charlie leaves." How does Charlie enter? How does Charlie
exit? Make it a *character thing* by being more *specific*.

Let every description of action characterize your character,
and/or create mood or emotion, and/or dramatize the action.

```
Charlie silently slithers in.
```

```
Charlie staggers into the bathroom and,
on his third try, kicks the door shut.
```

THREE, FIVE, OR NINE ACTS?

QUESTION
What are your thoughts regarding nine acts versus three acts?

ANSWER
Well, a nine-act story still has three main parts. It has a beginning middle and end, just like a three-act story. Some screenwriters like to think in terms of four acts—each about equal length. They still have a beginning (which focuses on establishing story, characters, and situation), middle (mostly concerned with complications and a rising conflict, culminating in some kind of crisis), and end (the showdown and denouement). Shakespeare used five acts, and even when he was in love, there was a beginning, middle (Acts 2, 3, and 4), and end. Most TV MOWs (movies-of-the-week) have seven acts. The first act is the beginning, and the last two are usually the end.

Basic dramatic structure is about the same for everyone. Now, how you specifically apply it to the content of your story requires some creativity and skill, and how you present the content of your story so that it is dramatic and compelling also requires some creativity and skill.

AND SITUATION COMEDY?

QUESTION
...But isn't a situation comedy just two acts?

ANSWER
Yes, it has a teaser, the first act, the second act, and a tag or epilogue. However, it still has a beginning, middle, and end. The way it differs from a screenplay is that the middle is divided by a pinch that is one of the following: 1) The funniest thing in the sitcom that makes us anticipate more hilarity while the commercial plays, 2) A very serious and dramatic turning point that makes us wonder what is going to happen next while the commercial plays, or 3) A funny twist that makes us wonder what is going to happen next while the commercial plays.

May what happens next involve a six-figure contract. Good luck and keep writing.

A PROFESSIONAL LOOKING SCRIPT

QUESTION
How unprofessional can I be in formatting? Do I have to have everything exactly right?

ANSWER
If your story is wonderful, then the reader will overlook many other things. Then again, the reader may never read your script if he is turned off by those "other things" when he glances through your script. Obviously, the story is the most important thing, but formatting is important. In marketing, we call this packaging. Packaging is important in selling the product.

To give you a straight answer, if the errors in formatting are minimal, you will probably be okay. Keep in mind that different people in the biz have different ideas of what correct formatting is. However, if you follow the rules of *spec formatting* as best you can, you will be just fine.

HOW LONG A SCENE?

QUESTION
I've read in various articles and heard from a wide variety of industry professionals that a scene should take up no more than three to four pages (exceptions granted). How many times can this rule be successfully broken?

ANSWER
Any scene length is fine *if* it works. The first sword fight scene in *The Princess Bride* is ten pages. Nevertheless, I usually recommend "challenging" any scene over 2-3 pages. Sometimes you need long scenes, but often you don't. There isn't a magic number, since it depends on the scene, the context, and what the scene accomplishes.

However, many scenes can be streamlined and improved if you will give them a hard look. For example, can you start the scene later in the scene without losing what is important to the scene? If so, omit some of the beginning. Are you being redundant in your scene? If so, you can do some condensing. Does your scene end strong, wanting us to see what happens next? In other words, is the scene compelling? If so, then you're probably okay.

THAT FIRST DRAFT

QUESTION
I tend to write the action for each scene as I visualize it "on screen." Sometimes formatting seems to get in the way of this creative process. Any tricks?

ANSWER
In your first draft, write it just the way you see it in your mind, and use any format you'd like. Forget all the rules. Just get

something down on paper. Write from the heart. Go ahead and have fun! Then, in your second draft, conform what you have to proper spec form.

THE OPENING HOOK

QUESTION
When writing my script, should I focus on catching the reader's attention quickly or on the quality and content of the story?

ANSWER
Both. That does not mean that you must open with a car chase and explosion, but you must pull the reader into the story.

RIGHT FIRST, WRITE SECOND

QUESTION
You say get the right or rights first before writing a sequel or adaptation, but my instructor says write the movie, and then worry about the rights. Why different views?

ANSWER
My advice assumes you are writing to *sell*.

For example, let's say you write a sequel to the most recent Indiana Jones flick. Who are you going to sell your sequel to? Well, you can only sell it to the people who own the rights. And since they have you over a barrel, they can say if they choose, "We'll give you a grand for your script; take it or leave it." Do you see that you are in a weak negotiating position?

Of course, if your script is absolutely brilliant, then maybe they will be willing to pay you your price. That could happen, so your instructor could be right. Just keep in mind that you have only one buyer when you write a sequel.

In the case of an adaptation, if you are already emotionally invested in a work that you have already adapted, and the seller of the rights senses that, then you place yourself in a weak negotiating position. My advice derives from my desire to place you in a strong negotiating position.

AGENT RESPONSE TIME

QUESTION
How long does it take for an agent to respond?

ANSWER
Forever.   Actually, it can take several months. Give the agent at least a month before doing any kind of follow-up.   During that follow-up call, ask when you can expect a response, and then wait until that time period has lapsed before calling again.

SITCOM DIALOGUE

QUESTION
I want to write an episode for a situation comedy. Is the formatting for dialogue the same as in feature length scripts?

ANSWER
No. Sitcom dialogue is double-spaced and is different in other ways. Perhaps, a comparison would be helpful.

What follows is how a speech would be written in standard spec screenplay format.

```
                    GROUCHO
        The other day I shot an elephant
        in my pajamas.
                (flicking his cigar)
        How the elephant got in my
        pajamas I don't know.
```

What follows is the same speech written for a situation comedy.

```
                    GROUCHO

        The other day I shot an elephant

        in my pajamas.  (FLICKING HIS

        CIGAR.)  How the elephant got

        in my pajamas I don't know.
```

As you can see, there is a big difference between the two examples.

One reason the TV sitcom style emphasizes dialogue is that a sitcom is actually a two-act stage play shot for TV. Usually, in a TV situation comedy, the emphasis is on dialogue, not on action. Often, there are only one or two sets for a sitcom series.

If you wish to write for a specific sitcom, you will first want to verify that scripts are being considered for that show. You will also want to see how scripts for that show are formatted. That's because there are slight differences from series to series.

EXITS AND ENTRANCES

QUESTION
Is capitalization of entrances and exits passé? Example:
SHARON EXITS. I want to keep things "clean and lean," but
can't decide if the CAPSs are a help or a burden to the reader.

ANSWER
Let me respond first for screenwriters, and second for TV
sitcom writers.

In screenwriting, no CAPS are required for entrances and
exits. In a scene, simply describe the action of the entrance or
exit and who is involved in that action.

For example, if someone enters the scene or exits the scene,
and it's important to point that out, then do so. But don't write
SHARON EXITS. Doing so tells us almost nothing about
Sharon or the story. Instead, describe <u>how</u> she exits to
characterize her, or to reveal her feelings or attitude, or to
reveal something of her character. Here are three examples:

```
As Sharon waves goodbye, she steps
backwards and trips through the doorway.

Sharon slams the door behind her.

Sharon steps triumphantly through the
doorway.
```

See more examples on page 89.

In a situation comedy, all narrative description is capitalized,
and entrances and exits are underscored.

```
SHARON WAVES GOODBYE AND EXITS.
```

HOUR-LONG TV SHOWS

QUESTION
Is an hour-long TV show formatted the same way as sitcoms?

ANSWER
No. An hour-long TV show is formatted in standard spec script format, just like a feature length script. The only difference is that you label the teaser, four acts, and tag (or epilogue). Some hour-long TV shows are written in five acts instead of four.

Always get a copy of a script for the TV show you wish to write to see the formatting nuances of that particular show.

An MOW (movie of the week), by the way, is usually written in seven acts, but you usually do not need to delineate the acts in a *spec* MOW script.

SHOW ME THE MONEY

QUESTION
I heard the real money is in TV, but how can that be when some screenwriters make over a million for a screenplay.

ANSWER
Most established screenwriters are not making millions per script. But most established TV writers not only make six figures, they make it year after year. It is true that there is a lot of consistent money in TV writing.

The downside is you will work long hours to make that money. I have a friend who writes for a sitcom, who said he would love to take a break from TV, but he can't give up the big bucks.

Whatever venue you choose to write for, in order to make any bucks at all, you need to keep writing. Good luck!

IT'S STILL THE SAME OLD STORY

QUESTION
What is the difference between SAME and CONTINUOUS?

ANSWER
It depends on whom you talk to. Usually, the term CONTINUOUS is added to a master scene heading to indicate that it follows the previous scene without any break in time. Here is an example.

```
INT. CASTLE - DAY

Squire Hermagilde spots dozens of red
knights approaching the castle.  Scared
speechless, he lunges through the open
doorway.

INT. STAIRWELL - CONTINUOUS

He races down the stairs and through
another doorway.

EXT. DRAWBRIDGE - CONTINUOUS

He pulls the drawbridge chain hand over
hand, drawing the bridge up, just as the
red knights arrive at the moat.
```

The term SAME is usually used in the same way.

```
EXT. STAIRWELL - SAME
```

Some people use the term SAME to indicate a scene that happens at precisely the same time as the previous scene; in other words, simultaneously. However, those occasions are extremely rare. (See pages 165-166 for more examples.)

In summary, for virtually all intents and purposes, the terms CONTINUOUS and SAME are synonymous.

DAY OR NIGHT

QUESTION
I like to flow scenes together, and the suffixes DAY and NIGHT often become redundant. For that reason I try to use headings and sub-headings to avoid repetition of DAY and NIGHT. For instance:

```
INT. KITCHEN - DAY

Darrin heads out to the

BACKYARD

to find Ann resting in a hammock.
```

ANSWER
First of all, it's okay to omit the terms DAY or NIGHT from a heading *if* it's already obvious what the time of day is and *if* that time of day has not changed since the previous scene.

In your example above, the BACKYARD is not part of the KITCHEN, so a secondary heading (BACKYARD) is impossible. In other words, the BACKYARD is another master location that requires a master scene heading. However, you could end that second master scene heading with CONTINUOUS or SAME (instead of DAY), since one scene follows right on the heels of the other. Therefore, this would be correct:

```
INT. KITCHEN - DAY

Darrin saunters to the door.

EXT. BACKYARD - CONTINUOUS

Darrin finds Ann resting in a hammock.
```

FOLLOW-UP QUESTION
In what situation could I use secondary headings?

ANSWER
You can use secondary headings when you cut from one (master) location to a location that is within or part of that master location. Let's borrow an earlier scene, and re-format it to illustrate this point.

```
INT. CASTLE - DAY

Squire Hermagilde spots dozens of red
knights approaching the castle.  Scared,
he races through the doorway and down the

STAIRWELL

through another doorway to the

DRAWBRIDGE

where he tugs at the drawbridge chain,
and pulls up the bridge just as the red
knights arrive at the moat.
```

Since the **STAIRWELL** and **DRAWBRIDGE** are both part of

the master location (the CASTLE), they can be used secondary headings.

GOING UNDERGROUND

QUESTION
Much of my script takes place underground in a cavern that has its own continuous light, and time of day doesn't matter. In the slug line [heading], should I use DAY or NIGHT? Example: INT. CAVERN - DAY.

ANSWER
You probably don't need DAY or NIGHT for the situation you describe.

SPECIAL WORDS AND ITALICS

QUESTION
If there are words in the action or dialogue segments that are unusual, such as the name of an extra terrestrial civilization called the *Barkuda*, or the Latin term for African lion, *panthera leo*, is it okay to italicize the words for a reader, so that the reader will know that the words are special and not typos?

If so, would one italicize every occurrence of the word(s), or just the first?

ANSWER
Do not bold or italicize anything in a spec screenplay. The one exception is you may italicize (or underscore) foreign words (such as *panthera leo*).

As a general rule, when you want to emphasize anything in a

screenplay, such as a word or phrase of dialogue or a sentence of narrative description, <u>underscore</u> the word, phrase or sentence. Do this only rarely.

If you wish to emphasize an important sound, use all-CAPS. Although it is no longer necessary to place sounds in all-CAPS, you may emphasize important sounds if you wish.

ACRONYMS, ABBREVIATIONS, AND NUMBERS

QUESTION
Would you please tell me if it is professional/acceptable to use acronyms when writing a spec script? For example, may I use MCC for Mobile Command Center?

ANSWER
Acronyms are fine. Just make sure the reader knows what they stand for.

The main thing is to be absolutely clear so that the reader does not get confused. You don't want a reader wondering what MCC stands for.

FOLLOW-UP QUESTION
Can I abbreviate words; for example, hwy for highway?

ANSWER
In the words of William Safire, "Don't abbrev" (and, while you're at it, "don't use no double negatives" neither).

Do not abbreviate regular words like highway. It comes across as sloppy writing. In dialogue speeches particularly, you must write out the words.

FOLLOW-UP QUESTION
What about numbers?

ANSWER
All numbers (except years and proper names [such as C3PO])
should be written out as words in speeches.

SEX CHANGES

QUESTION
When my heroine is disguised as a man, how do I refer to that
heroine in action/description—as a "he" or a "she"?

ANSWER
As a "she." In virtually all situations, refer to your character
by her real identity, even when she is posing as a man.

THE "FALLING IN LOVE" MONTAGE

QUESTION
I'm at the point in my romantic comedy script where the two
characters get together and fall in love. I want to show the
audience that two months go by in the characters' lives and in
the things they do; that is, go on a picnic, go to the beach,
attend parties, etc.

Usually, in actual movies, there is music during this section.
How do I write it down so that the producer/director knows
what sort of sequence I am after.

ANSWER
You are referring to the MONTAGE. Use the specific shots
of your montage to show "passage of time" or "falling in love"
(or any other concept). Here's an example.

MONTAGE - JIM & SUZY FALL IN LOVE

-- At a picnic in the park, Jim and Suzy wolf down an entire chicken in record time. Their affectionate countenances are smeared with chicken fat.

-- Jim (now with two-months growth of beard) and Suzy jog along the beach until they come upon a beached whale. Together, they push the huge mammal back into the ocean. The whale waves its tail in grateful thanks. Jim and Suzy wave back.

And so on. You did say this was a comedy, right? :-)

In terms of passage of time, I used a beard in the above example, but you will not need to be so obvious. Normally, show passage of time by how the relationship grows or deteriorates.

A classic example is the breakfast montage in *Citizen Kane*. Obviously, time is passing. In both *A Man for All Seasons* and *A Beautiful Mind,* there are short montages of the seasons changing.

Incidentally, you should not indicate music in your montage. The director, composer, or producer will see an opportunity to insert a hit song. Your job is to keep writing.

I SEE THE LIGHT

QUESTION
Say you're writing a scene where somebody is seeing something mentally (presumably the people with him or her wouldn't see whatever the image was). You want the

audience to see what the character is seeing as well. How would you write that?

For example, there was a recent TV movie that aired called *Living With the Dead* with Ted Danson. In several scenes, the main character sees visions in his head, and we the audience see the same visions. How would that be written? Would we need a whole new scene heading for each mental image, even though we really haven't left the first scene?

ANSWER
Let's assume that your character's name is Dame Nostra. Just write what the audience sees, and label it clearly. You would format it just as you would a flashback or a dream, but instead of DAME NOSTRA'S DREAM or FLASHBACK as a heading (slug line), your heading would be DAME NOSTRA'S IMAGINATION OR THE DAME'S VISION, or something similar to that. For example, if she sees the woods at night, you might write:

```
DAME NOSTRA'S VISION - THE WOODS AT NIGHT
```

And then describe what Dame Nostra and the audience see. The main thing is to clearly communicate to the reader what is happening on the movie screen.

I HEAR THE PHONE

QUESTION
What is the best way to cross cut a telephone conversation that cuts back and forth between two characters.

ANSWER
I think you want the INTERCUT. Simply establish the two locations and write out the telephone conversation as follows:

INT. MARY'S KITCHEN - NIGHT

Mary paces nervously, then punches numbers on her phone.

INT. DARIN'S CAR - SAME

Darin drives through the rain, looking depressed. His cell phone rings.

INTERCUT - TELEPHONE CONVERSATION

> MARY
> Come back.

> DARIN
> What? Now?

> MARY
> Yes. Please.

> DARIN
> Give me one good reason.

> MARY
> You forgot your casserole bowl.

> DARIN
> I'll be right there.

Here's an alternate way to handle this.

INTERCUT - MARY'S KITCHEN/DARIN'S CAR

Mary paces nervously, then punches numbers on her phone.

Darin drives through the rain, looking
depressed. His cell phone rings.

And then write out the dialogue.

I SMELL A RAT

QUESTION
How does a writer denote in a spec screenplay the fact that a
character has a double identity, and is known to individual
characters under two separate identities? Example: a character
is known as BILL to one set of characters, but JIM to
another—do you type both BILL/JIM each time he speaks
dialogue in the screenplay? Bear in mind that the crux of the
story is that he appears as a good guy to one set of characters
and as a dirty rat to another set of characters.

ANSWER
You ask a good question, since it will be important to not
confuse the reader. Clarity is the overriding principle in cases
like this one. That is why you should normally use the same
name in your *character cue* throughout the screenplay. Thus,
I believe the best solution is the one you suggest. Refer to the
character as BILL/JIM in the dialogue *character cue*
whenever he speaks, as follows:

                    BILL/JIM
          What did you just call me?

Now if this character's true identity is BILL and that's
established early, then consider referring to him as BILL (in
the character cue) throughout the entire screenplay, even
though some characters might call him something else (in
dialogue).   That is what happens in NORTH BY
NORTHWEST. We know that Cary Grant is Roger Thornhill,

even though most people call him by another name during the majority of the movie. Thus, the character cue would show THORNHILL throughout the entire script.

I'M OKAY, YOU'RE OKAY

QUESTION
OK or Okay? I have an editor friend of mine who keeps correcting my "OKs"! She says they need to be spelled out as "okay," but I think "OK" is acceptable. Please help.

ANSWER
Your editor is okay. "Okay" is a word. "OK" is an acronym that goes back two centuries. It stands for "Oll Korrect." Thus, it's not only okay to write "okay," it's also OK.

MARGIN CALL

QUESTION
As I understand it, the right margin of a script should be at one-half inch; but I have seen the right margin of some scripts at anywhere from a half inch to 1.5 inches. What is correct?

ANSWER
They all are.

The right margin is normally at one-half inch to one inch. However, if your screenplay length is a bit short and you need to add pages, you might consider creating more white space on each of the pages—that's one reason you might have a right margin of more than an inch. It's your call. However, the following always applies: Left margin should be 1.5 inches, right margin should be no shorter than one-half inch, and the right margin should be ragged.

CALLING THE SHOTS

QUESTION
I find it difficult to write without including camera shots. In the following two examples, a camera shot is needed, but which would be more acceptable?

```
EXT. HOUSE - DAY

CLOSE SHOT

Ty's hand grabs the doorknob.
```

Or, would this be better:

```
EXT. HOUSE - DAY

CLOSE ON Ty's hand grabbing the doorknob.
```

ANSWER
I am not seeing a reason for either camera direction. The following would be better, and it implies a CLOSE UP.

```
EXT. HOUSE - DAY

Ty's hand grabs the doorknob.
```

BUT HOW *MUCH* DETAIL?

QUESTION
I know I shouldn't direct the director, so I try to keep the dialogue and description lean. But where do I draw the line between too little detail and too much detail? Should I write

```
Molly cries.
```

Or...

```
Molly cries.  Her body shakes, hands
tremble, face turns red.
```

ANSWER
This is an important question because, as writers, we sometimes wonder where this fine line lies. Your second example adds drama and interest. If Molly is an important character, the reader will more readily identify with your second example. But don't go beyond that and describe how her tears like prisms refract the light streaming through the window, creating chromatic scales of sad colors.

The key is to provide details that move the story forward, add dimension to your characters, add atmosphere (be careful here), and so on.

It follows that you don't need to include every incidental action. For example, don't write "He lays the coffee cup on the edge of the table." No one cares where he lays the coffee cup <u>unless</u> he is going to spill it later, or it contains a laxative. Focus on story and character elements.

If your character enters a classroom, just describe it as an ordinary classroom. We do not need to know about the windows unless someone is going to come through those windows. We don't need to know what kinds of desks or chairs are in the room unless our character cannot fit into his/her desk. Again, focus on story and character elements.

AND THE MUSIC?

QUESTION
Shouldn't I indicate when the orchestra plays?

ANSWER

No. Your great writing establishes the mood for each scene. This is where the music composer should get his cues.

ACTION AND PARENTHETICALS

QUESTION

Is the following example correct?

```
                    JACK
          (grabs Jill by the
          hand)
     Could sure use some water,
     my dear.
          (a beat; starts up
          the hill)


                    JILL
          (snatches the bucket
          out of his hand)
     Sounds like a good idea, Jack.
          (swings bucket around
          and around as they near
          the well)
```

ANSWER

Action should be written as action, unless that action can be described in just a few words (tipping his hat). Also, do not end a dialogue block with a parenthetical; end it with dialogue. Finally, the dialogue in the example above is stiff; let's make it more natural. At the same time, we'll try to give the scene a little more movement. Here is my revision.

```
Jack shows Jill his empty bucket.
```

                        JACK
        Water?

Jill snatches the bucket.

                        JILL
        Race ya.

She swings the bucket around as they
gallop to the well.

CALIFORNIA DREAMIN'

QUESTION
I want to be a screenwriter, but I cannot move to L.A. What
do I do?

ANSWER
You don't have to move to L.A. It helps, but it is not
necessary. Writers break in from outside of L.A. all the time.
Just keep writing.

TIME JUMPS

QUESTION
My opening scene shows a small child being tended to by his
mother and three other women. This scene takes place in the
past, and we soon meet all of these characters again 25 years
later. How do I describe everyone in my opening scene in
comparison to how they will be described a few scenes later
when they are older? Is he a YOUNG VINCENT? And do I
describe them again later?

ANSWER
Yes and yes. Call him "YOUNG VINCENT, four years old," or whatever his age is. And then when you cut to 25 years later, call him "VINCENT, now 29." And then describe him just as you would if this were the first scene in the movie.

In the character cue, likewise, you would refer to him as YOUNG VINCET and VINCENT.

TIME STANDS STILL

QUESTION
In my scene, a young newlywed couple is at a park among guests, cutting the cake. The next scene shows the same couple 13 years later, watching the tape of their wedding at the park (the previous scene). What would be the correct way to write this?

ANSWER
There are many correct ways. Let's look at just one. I think the key to the transition will be to cut from one action to that same action on the video tape.

```
EXT. PARK - DAY

Mary takes the knife and, with John's
hand on hers, cuts the wedding cake.

INT. HOUSE - DAY

On a TV screen, the same Mary cuts the
cake.

Together on a couch, John and Mary watch
the video contentedly, children at their
feet.
```

If you want to be clearer about the jump in time, you could mention "13 years" in dialogue, or double space and write:

```
SUPER: "13 YEARS LATER."
```

MONTAGE AND LOCATION

QUESTION
What is the correct format for a montage that has a series of scenes at different locations, but no dialogue?

ANSWER
There are many correct ways to format a MONTAGE or SERIES OF SHOTS. It all depends on your purpose.

Generally, a MONTAGE is used to describe a series of images that convey a concept, such as passage of time or falling in love.

The SERIES OF SHOTS is for a straight narrative, a chronology of events. Naturally, the two are often used interchangeably.

What follows is standard format for the MONTAGE.

```
MONTAGE - JOHN WAITS FOR MARY

-- John glances at the waiting room
clock. It says, "10:00."

-- He stares at a door, glances back at
the clock - "10:30."

-- He paces the room nervously -- 11:00.
The door opens and Mary exits the
bathroom.
```

In your question, you describe a series of locations. So let's format a MONTAGE that emphasizes location.

```
MONTAGE - JOHN FALLS FOR MARY

-- AT A RESTAURANT -- John and Mary
exchange caring glances over a glass of
wine.

-- AT THE BEACH -- John and Mary frolic
in the sun.

-- ON MARY'S BALCONY -- John kisses Mary,
then falls back over the railing,
flailing his arms.
```

Of course, you don't necessarily have to CAP your locations. For example, you could write:

```
-- At a restaurant, John and Mary
exchange caring glances over a glass of
wine.
```

And so on. Whatever format you decide to use, be consistent.

Let's look at standard format for a SERIES OF SHOTS.

```
SERIES OF SHOTS -- John gets even.

A) John lifts a gun from his desk drawer.

B) John strides down a sidewalk.

C) Mary answers the door.  John pulls the
trigger.  A stream of water hits Mary in
the face.
```

As you can see, there is very little difference between the MONTAGE and SERIES OF SHOTS. In both cases, you start with an informative heading, and then list shots in a way that best suits your purpose. The main thing is to follow the basic form and strive for clarity so that the reader can follow.

FADE OUT

QUESTION
After fading to black at the end of my screenplay, I want to do a succession of fade in/fade out captions listing the eventual fates of certain characters. How would I format this?

ANSWER
I suggest that you use a series of SUPERs. The reader will know that each fades in and fades out over a black screen.

FADE TO BLACK.

```
SUPER:

          "SLICK WILLY LATER WENT ON
          TO BECOME PRESIDENT OF THE
          UNITED STATES."
```

And so on.

TIME LAPSES

QUESTION
I'm stumped. I want to show a time lapse from day to night for a story reason. A character, Jimmy, parks a Chevy automobile next to a building; someone is locked in the trunk (established in an earlier scene). I want to focus on the Chevy

while everything around it changes. Jimmy will stand by the car and then disappear. The sequence will end in a light rain for the next scene. How do I format that?

ANSWER
The fact that you have a "story reason" for this time lapse is what prompted me to respond. I would use a format that is similar to the MONTAGE. How about something like this?

```
TIME LAPSE

The Chevy stays in the same place as
everything around it changes.

-- Jimmy disappears.

-- The day evolves into night as lights
go on, then out, in the building behind
the car.

-- Two teenagers gather around the Chevy,
then disappear.

-- A light rain drizzles.

EXT. STREET - MORNING

The only sound is the rain on the Chevy.
And then the usual sounds of morning
become apparent.
```

THE BEAT GOES ON

QUESTION
At what point in a character's dialogue pause or break is it necessary to insert a BEAT?

ANSWER

The use of "beat" is legitimate, but I suggest that you don't use it to indicate a pause, but instead insert a bit of action, a gesture, or a facial expression. Doing that will not only imply the pause (or beat) you want, but it will also reveal something about the character and/or the story. For example, this is what I typically see in unsold spec screenplays.

```
                    JIM
          You know...
                (beat)
          ...I'll have to kill you.
```

A beat.

They exchange glances.

Another beat.

This is what I would prefer to see.

```
                    JIM
          You know...
                (looking nervous)
          ...I'll have to kill you.
```

Jim's hand shakes as he reaches into his coat.

Drew smiles confidently, holds Jim's gaze.

He glances down. Can't take the heat.

The second version tells me something about character and story, while at the same time implying a pause or beat.

KILLER CORNBREAD

QUESTION
After watching movies like *The Ring* and *Identity*, I was wondering how much of the script actually turns into the visuals we see on the screen. Does the writer simply provide his version with dialogue and minor details and the director creates his own vision for the screen? My main question is when writing, how much description of key actions can the writer use throughout the script if it is relevant to the story?

ANSWER
If an action moves the story forward or adds to character, then write it. A spec script should contain specific details, but only those details that are important to the story or which reveal character. For example, here is a small detail from a script.

```
Selma nibbles at her cornbread.
```

Normally, this incidental detail is unnecessary. It's not important enough to keep. On the other hand, if there is rat killer in that cornbread, then it is an important detail that should be in the script.

If there is a key fight scene, describe the scene so that the reader can visualize it. You don't have to choreograph the fight, but you need to describe most of the blows and tumbles. What the director chooses to use or not use is up to her.

Remember, your job is to give the script reader goose bumps, tense up her muscles, make her laugh, or bring tears to her eyes. You can't do that with general or vague details such as "They fight," or "they make love." At the same time, don't add unnecessary details. Remember, the more you write, the more you will get a sense of how much detail to add. So keep writing.

SPACED OUT

QUESTION
Although I don't use a software package for writing my screenplays (I use Word), I strictly follow the formatting conventions. The other day on a screenwriter's message forum, I read that the lines-per-page standard is 54 lines. To date I've never read that in any formatting book. Further, the message stated that Microsoft Word's default single line spacing results in only 50 lines per page. Applying that formatting scheme to my 106-page screenplay, it shrunk to 96 pages. Can you clarify this "lines per page" standard?

ANWSWER
Anywhere between 50-55 lines is okay, but who's counting? I don't know any readers who do. Line spacing is less crucial to a spec script than to a shooting script. However, if a reader looks at your script and the lines seem crammed together, then that's a negative, so stay within that 50-55 lines range. Most screenwriting software formats at about 54 lines per page.

Incidentally, now you know what to do if your script is too long or too short—adjust the line spacing. ☺

A TRIPLE DOUBLE

QUESTION
Do you double-space before master scene headings or triple-space?

ANSWER
It's your choice, and that's the *underlying theme* of this column. There is often more than one "correct" formatting technique that you can apply to most screenwriting situations. Keep writing!

THE STORYTELLER

QUESTION
My script is pretty much told in flashback, so would I format that as FLASHBACK, write the rest of the story until I reach the point where we come out of the flashback, and then write END OF FLASHBACK or BACK TO PRESENT DAY?

ANSWER
It appears that you are using the "storyteller device." In other words, most of your movie is one long flashback, as is the case with *Saving Private Ryan.*

Therefore, instead of a flashback, use a SUPER (short for *superimpose*) that identifies the year that we flash back to.

Here's an example that assumes your character is a 71-year-old man at the beginning of the movie.

```
John's eyes get misty.  He looks off into
the distance.

EXT. SAN FRANCISCO - DAY

An 18-year-old John stands at a busy
intersection.

SUPER: "San Francisco, 1950."
```

At the end of the movie, you will return to PRESENT DAY.

NAUGHTY WORDS

QUESTION
I am writing a script, and I want to know how I would write

"shit" as in "and then a bird shits on the windshield."   Or should I use crap, poop, or something else?

ANSWER

How about *defecates*?   The word is not as important as the action.   Make this visually interesting to the reader.   Here's one possible example:

```
A raven releases a white bomb on the
windshield -- SPLAT!  The windshield
wiper smears the payload across the
window.
```

Let me address your underlying question: Is it okay to use "naughty words" in a screenplay?   My general response is to take the high road when writing *narrative description*, but to write what the characters say in *dialogue*.

Of course, if you are writing a "low comedy," then you might want to maintain that tone in your narrative description as well as in your dialogue.

Finally, don't use "language" just to demonstrate that you are hip; make sure all of your words contribute to the reading experience;   in other words, write clear, visual narrative description and crisp, original dialogue.

I once had an agent tell me a curious thing, and she was referring to dialogue.   She said, "Use less profanity and crude language in your script than you would expect to see in the completed movie."   She told me that a lot of "language" grates on a reader.   Since then, I have heard other professionals say the same thing.   I imagine with most it doesn't matter.

PHONE TALK

QUESTION
I am having trouble with one of my scenes and I need help. There are two characters. One character is on screen, and the other is at another location on the phone. Should I use (O.C.) or (O.S.)?

Furthermore, when the two characters are speaking to each other, should I only establish the parenthetical (O.C.) or (O.S.) once in association with that character or throughout the character's dialogue in the scene?

ANSWER
Let's answer the first question first. Don't use (O.C.) at all; it has fallen out of use.

It appears as though your second character is in a separate location and we only hear his voice through the phone. In that case, his dialogue is "voiced over" (V.O.).

Use (O.S.) if a character is in the scene at the location, but is "off screen." In other words, use (O.S.) if we don't see her on the silver screen, but she is at the scene location.

To answer your second question, use (V.O.) in every instance that the character's phone dialogue is "voiced over," and use (O.S.) for every instance that the character's dialogue is spoken "off screen." Be clear. Have fun. And keep writing.

SOUNDING OFF

QUESTION
I understand that SOUNDS are sometimes written in CAPS, but I have also seen characters (after their initial introduction),

places, and actions put in CAPS. For example:

1. The door swings open and BILL saunters
into the room with a handful of QUARTERS.

2. The CAR dims its lights and turns into
the CONVENIENCE STORE LOT.

3. The boy STRIKES his father and FLEES
on a bike.

What is your opinion on CAPS being used in this manner? I
see it all the time, yet I've never read anything about it in
formatting books or the like.

ANSWER
The reason you see it a lot is because you are (likely) reading
shooting scripts. The reason you seldom see it in formatting
books is because they provide instruction for *spec* scripts. A
spec script is one written to sell; a shooting script is written for
the shoot.

In a shooting script, sounds and props are usually CAPPED so
that the production manager can easily break down the script
(prepare a shooting schedule, make lists of props and sound
effects, and so on). On occasion, you may find a shooting
script where all character names are CAPPED so that they can
be tracked in the breakdown.

Unfortunately, many developing writers use these shooting
script conventions in their spec scripts. That makes their spec
scripts more difficult to read.   Let's review your three
examples in view of generally accepted spec writing
conventions.

1. If this is not Bill's first appearance in the screenplay, his
name should not appear in all-CAPS. The QUARTERS are a

prop and shouldn't be CAPPED in a spec script. In fact, as a general rule, nouns are not placed in all-CAPS. (The exception is the name of a character when he or she first appears in the screenplay.) Thus, this sentence should be written as follows:

```
The door swings open and Bill saunters
into the room with a handful of quarters.
```

2. The word "car" should not appear in all-CAPS. The CONVENIENCE STORE LOT appears to be a new location. If so, it should be written as a heading (slug line). If the convenience store lot is a secondary location that is part of the master scene location, then this sentence would be written as follows:

```
The car dims its lights and turns into
the

CONVENIENCE STORE LOT

where it slows to a stop.
```

If the convenience store lot is a new master scene location, then the sentence should be revised as follows.

```
The car dims its lights and turns.

EXT. CONVENIENCE STORE LOT - CONTINUOUS

The car slows to a stop in the parking
lot.
```

You may be wondering what the difference is between a master scene heading and a secondary heading. The master scene heading presents a master location. A secondary heading presents a location that is part of the master location.

Here's an example.

```
INT. CONVENIENCE STORE - NIGHT

A man wearing a werewolf Halloween mask
enters.

AT THE COUNTER

the clerk freezes in fear.

IN THE AISLE

a young couple faint together.

AT THE COUNTER

the masked man opens a large paper sack.

                    MASKED MAN
          Trick or treat.
```

In the above example, you can clearly see that the counter and aisle are secondary locations that are part of the primary or master location (the store).

Even though the above example is in correct format, the scene doesn't have to be written that way. What follows would also be correct and probably preferred.

```
INT. CONVENIENCE STORE - NIGHT

A man wearing a werewolf Halloween mask
enters.

The clerk at the counter freezes in fear.
```

```
In one of the aisles, a young couple
faint together.

The masked man steps towards the clerk
and opens a Halloween sack.

                 MASKED MAN
          Trick or treat.
```

Notice, in the above scene, that there is no word in the narrative description written in all-CAPS.

3. In your third example on page 124, the CAPS emphasize action and imply sound effects. However, the words "strikes" and "flees" do not need be placed in all-CAPS in a spec script.

Although you are no longer required to CAP sounds in a spec script, it is okay to CAP important sounds, if you wish. So you might want to CAP the word "strike." Here's what I would probably write:

```
The boy strikes his father and flees on a
bike.
```

MORE CAPS

QUESTION
After a character is introduced as BURLY COP [in narrative description], what is the correct form for the remainder of the script? For instance, I have seen it written [in narrative description] as Burly Cop, burly cop, and even burly Cop. After reading hundreds of screenplays and numerous books, I have yet to find a clear-cut answer for this.

ANSWER
Burly Cop.

LOOK WHO'S PRAYING

QUESTION
How do I write one dialogue speech for three characters to say at the same time? For example, I have a scene where three characters say the same prayer at the same time.

ANSWER
I can best answer this with an example.

>   LARRY, MOE & CURLY
>   Now I lay me down to sleep/Pray
>   the Lord my soul to keep.

Naturally, in the above example, I could have written "at the same time," "together," or "in unison" as a parenthetical to be absolutely clear. Personally, I see that as redundant, but it would be okay.

Now if someone starts saying something, and the other begins before the first has finished, then that overlapping dialogue is written as follows:

>   CURLY
>   Now I roll down my covers --
>
>   MOE
>   (overlapping)
>   -- Not until you say your
>   prayers, ya knucklehead.

POETIC LICENSE

QUESTION
How do I separate lines in a stanza of a poem?

ANSWER
Use a slash. See the example above of the Three Stooges praying in unison.

WHERE TO PUT THE ACTION

QUESTION
I just finished an existing TV drama script and noticed something about my style for the first time. Sometimes I write a character's action on the action line [as narrative description], and sometimes I do it under the character's name itself [as a parenthetical, or actor's instruction]. Which is correct and, if they both are, can you have examples of both throughout your script, or should you just stick to one style?

ANSWER
If the action only takes a few words to describe, it's okay to write it either way—in narrative description or as a parenthetical.

```
                    ALBERT
               (tipping his hat)
          It's been a long time.

Loretta slaps his face.

                    LORETTA
          Not long enough.
```

As you can see, it is okay to use both styles in your screenplay, as I did in the example above. However, any action that takes more than a few words to describe should be written as narrative description only.

```
Loretta sucker punches Albert, then
pushes him into a mud puddle.
```

```
                    LORETTA
          How low can you get?
```

THE WRYLY FACTOR

QUESTION
At a recent conference, I heard many contradictory statements about formatting. Some say all of the action should be written in parentheticals [often referred to as wrylies] since producers only read the dialogue, and some say that there should be no parentheticals at all. Could you help?

ANSWER
It's true there are producers in town who only read dialogue, but that does not mean that they read the wrylies too, nor does it mean that *all* producers only read dialogue.

Keep in mind that before a producer reads your script, a professional reader reads it from beginning to end. Finally, when a production company gets serious about a script, then several people in the company may end up reading it. So don't be unduly concerned about how much of your script will get read. You cannot control that. What you can control is what you write.

Use wrylies sparingly. If there are too many, then a reader is likely not to take them too seriously. Their main purpose is to clarify the subtext when the subtext is not already apparent. For example, if a character says "I love you" in a sarcastic way, and it is not otherwise apparent that he would be sarcastic, then that's the time to use the parenthetical.

Too often, I see something like the following in a screenplay.

```
Kip is fighting mad.
```

```
              KIP
       (angrily shouting)
     I hate you!!!!
```

The above example says the same thing in three different ways. In this case, all that you need is the speech itself. Also, lose the exclamation points. Your speech should not look like a want ad.

Use a wryly to indicate action that can be described in a few words. I provided an example of that in the "Where to put the action" section above.

Use a wryly to indicate who the character is speaking to when that is not otherwise clear.

```
              MOE
          (to Curly)
     Not you, ya knucklehead.
```

If you follow this column, you already know that I discourage the use of the lifeless term "beat" to indicate a pause. I much prefer an adverbial, facial expression, or action that comments on either the story or the character while still implying a pause.

CALL WAITING

QUESTION
Concerning phone conversations, I was once told that the use of (O.S.) for a character on the phone is incorrect when writing a spec script. I was told to use this instead:

```
              MITCH (on phone)
     What are you doing?
```

```
                    JANICE (O.S., ON PHONE)
          Oh...just painting my toe nails.
```

ANSWER

You've been misinformed. The use of (O.S.) is incorrect because (O.S.) stands for OFF SCREEN, meaning that the character is in the scene (at the scene location), but cannot be seen on the silver screen. When a character is not at the scene location, then use (V.O.) for VOICE OVER.

In the case of your example, I assume that we can see Mitch, but that Janice is at some other location and that we hear her voice but don't see her. In that case, this would be correct:

```
Mitch holds the phone with one hand while
the other hand clips his toenails.

                    MITCH
          What are you doing?

                    JANICE (V.O.)
          Oh, just painting my toenails.
```

Concerning the phrase "on phone," it would work fine if we knew for sure what it meant. To some it means that the character is holding a phone to her ear. To others it means that the character's speech is voiced over. Since there can be confusion, I don't recommend you use it.

MORNING HAS BROKEN

QUESTION

I am taking a screenwriting course at my local junior college. I have the opening scene heading stating time of day as MORNING. My teacher scratched this out and replaced it with DAY, citing that the time of morning is assumed. She said that attaching so many different times of day to your scene headings will drive a producer crazy. What is the correct way? If my scene starts in the morning, should I put MORNING?

ANSWER
Your teacher makes a good point. As a general guideline, use DAY or NIGHT at the end of your master scene headings. For one thing, DAY and NIGHT are easier to shoot than MORNING and TWILIGHT. However, there are story situations when you need to emphasize the time of day (or night) and, in those cases, you should emphasize the time of day. So use your discretion.

LOST IN SPACE

QUESTION
What should a writer indicate for the time of day in the slug line [scene heading] when the time of day is not relevant? For example, if a scene takes place in space, such as on a spaceship, then the normal concepts of night and day do not apply. Similarly, a scene might take place in a subterranean cavern so deep that the time of day isn't relevant, since no sunlight can reach it.

ANSWER
There are two schools of thought on this. One is that the time of day is, as you say, irrelevant. Thus, a scene heading might be written as follows:

EXT. OUTER SPACE

And certainly, that is all you need for that scene heading. Another school of thought holds that since people behave as if it is night or day (sleeping or working, for example), those terms should be used in INTERIOR scenes, such as inside the spaceship or cave. Usually, that "assumed" time of day would already be obvious to the reader, so I lean towards the first school of thought—they usually aren't needed. However, I don't see a problem writing DAY or NIGHT, where doing so would clarify the situation.

MAY I INTRODUCE...?

QUESTION
I am unclear about how to introduce a character's name. I have read several books that state a character's name should not be revealed to the reader until that character speaks.

Yet there are several other books that state you can introduce a character's name with the character's description. Should main character names be introduced when they appear and minor character names introduced when they speak, or should the format remain consistent in some way?

ANSWER
One of the hallmarks of effective spec writing is the ability to be clear and *not* confuse the reader. The last thing you want is for an executive or agent to stop reading your script because they are confused. Thus, I favor simplicity and consistency over complexity and inconsistency.

As a reader, I want to know the character's name at the moment that character first appears. Naturally, there will be exceptions, but there should be a good "story" reason for those exceptions.

THIS STUFFING MAKES YOU A TURKEY

QUESTION
I have a question about the "script cardstock cover" and "title page" when sending a script to agents and producers. I have heard conflicting issues that the cardstock cover should remain blank, followed by the one page synopsis, followed by the title page. What is the correct format for professional presentation?

ANSWER
Blank cover stock, followed by the title page, followed by the script, followed by blank cover stock. That's it, unless an agent or producer specifically requests something else.

May I mention a pet peeve while we're on the subject? Please do not package your script with a padded envelope filled with stuffing that flies all over Kingdom Come when the envelope is opened. Sending your script in one of those will knock the stuffing out of that good first impression you want to make. If you want to use a padded envelope, use a bubble pack.

WHERE IN THE WORLD IS CARMEN?

QUESTION
If someone is writing a script that takes place in two separate geographical locations (e.g., Cabin on Cape Code and Tundra of Southern Chile), what is the best way to show the reader that the scene has not just changed minor locations but entire continents? Also, with regard to the last question, this is the kind of thing I have been doing with my headings.

```
INT. CHILE - PUNTA ARENAS - HOTEL -
CARMEN'S ROOM - EVENING
```

ANSWER

A scene heading should indicate the *specific* location of the scene, not everything you know about that location. Also, unless absolutely necessary, use DAY or NIGHT. Thus, I would revise your above example to the following:

INT. CARMEN'S HOTEL ROOM - DAY

Carmen's hotel room is the specific location of the scene. All the other information should come out in narrative description or previous scene headings.

Here's an example of what I mean.

EXT. CHILEAN TUNDRA - DAY

The vast Southern Chilean tundra extends for miles.

SUPER: "Southern Chile."

The city of Punta Arenas is visible in the distance.

EXT. PUNTA ARENAS HOTEL - SAME

A five-story red brick monolith dominates the smaller shops that surround it.

INT. CARMEN'S HOTEL ROOM - SAME

You could replace SAME with CONTINUOUS if you wish, or drop either term altogether since it's clearly evident that one scene follows on the heels of the other. It's your choice.

SOUNDS ARE SOUNDS, WORDS ARE WORDS

QUESTION
In my script, I have characters who make a lot of sounds, and sometimes I have written something like the following.

                    BOB
          (gasps)

                    LINDA
          (groans loudly)

So my question is, may I write parentheticals without any actual dialogue?

ANSWER
No. Dialogue consists of the actual words spoken by the character. Any other utterances are just sounds and should be written as narrative description, as follows:

Bob gasps.

Linda groans loudly.

The same is true of the sounds made by animals. Even though they may be communicating, write their barks and meows as sounds. If the sounds are crucial, and you want to emphasize them, it's okay to place them in CAPS, but it's not necessary that you do so.

FIRST APPEARANCES

QUESTION
I know that I should write in CAPS the name of any character when that character first appears in the screenplay. What if

you only hear their voice first? For example, my main character hears a little girl's scream but does not meet her until a later scene. Do I CAP "LITTLE GIRL" to ensure the voice belongs to the little girl that he will meet later? Or do I CAP only when she actually appears?

ANSWER
In this particular instance, I would write:

```
John hears the scream of a little girl.
```

The reason for that is to make it clear that the girl is not visible in the scene and that the scream is off screen. In the scene when she actually visually appears, CAP her name.

```
MELANIE, 8, glides into the room.
```

If you want to remind the reader of the scream that he read about earlier, then it's okay to introduce Melanie as follows:

```
MELANIE (8), the little girl that John
heard scream earlier, glides into the
room.
```

FIRST APPEARANCES FOLLOW-UP

QUESTION
When introducing a character, may I have the character speak first before he appears in the screenplay? Here's an example.

```
Mabel frantically glances up the stairs.

                    JONATHAN (O.S.)
          Are you all right?

Mabel quickly turns, startled.
```

```
JONATHAN, 17, looks menacing with a
baseball bat slung over his shoulder.

                    JONATHAN
          I'm Jonathan.
```

ANSWER
Yes you may, and your example above looks fine.

WHERE IS THE CAMERA?

QUESTION
There's a scene where we're standing by a lake. Then we're under the water looking up through the water at some children standing by the lake. How the heck should I slug that?

ANSWER
Since EXT. and INT. refer to where the camera is, and not to where the objects or people being shot are, I would think something like EXT. UNDERWATER would work. Then describe the action. How about something like this?

```
EXT. LAKE SHORE - DAY

The children form a circle by the lake.

EXT. UNDERWATER - SAME

While the others dance, Pam peers down
into the lake.
```

If you're thinking of a point-of-view situation, such as a monster watching the children from deep below the water's surface, just handle the second scene as follows:

```
EXT. UNDERWATER - SAME
```

```
An unseen lake monster watches the
dancing children.  Pam peers down into
the lake.
```

THROWING VOICES

QUESTION
What is the proper format for dialogue involving a ventriloquist and his dummy?

ANSWER
I think the clearest and most effective way to handle this is to treat the two as separate characters.

```
                    VENTRILOQUIST
          You're looking stiff today.


                        DUMMY
          I forgot to moisturize.
```

SPACING AFTER A PERIOD

QUESTION
What is the proper number of spaces after a period at the end of a sentence—one or two?

ANSWER
Although either is correct, my personal preference is for two, and I have two reasons. As spec screenwriters, we use a Courier font that imitates the PICA typewriter font of years gone by when the rule was two spaces. In addition, the extra space emphasizes that the sentence has ended. In other words, it makes sentences and paragraphs a bit easier to read.

JUST MY STYLE

QUESTION
Recently, I came across something regarding screenplays that talked about style and tone. Can you give me a brief explanation of these terms?

ANSWER
Style is a distinctive manner of expression, such as comedic style, formal style, folksy style, and so on. Most writers develop, usually subconsciously, a style of writing. For example, Shane Black often begins sentences with verbs. Here's an example from *The Last Boy Scout:*

```
He takes the [foot]ball on the run.
Tucks it under his arm.  Turns the
corner.  Picks up a blocker.
```

Style influences *tone*, which is the mood of the piece. In fact, the tone of a particular scene may imply a certain musical mood to the eventual composer of the musical soundtrack.

When famous cartoon character Snoopy writes "It's a dark and stormy night," he's trying to create a mood.

Often, writers adopt different styles for different scripts they are writing to influence the tone or mood of those scripts; and yet, everything they write will carry their imprint, something of their personal writing style.

SEEING DOUBLE

QUESTION
I'm a longtime subscriber of the magazine and I love to read your advice. Dr. Format is the first thing I read in every issue!

I have a character (let's call him Joe) who at times takes on the persona of a new character (Wayne). There is no other Wayne in the script. When Joe is pretending to be Wayne, should I still use his original name Joe when writing his dialogue, or should I use Wayne?

ANSWER
It's always a pleasure to answer questions from educated and discerning readers like yourself. (Oh, by the way, thanks for the compliment.)

Naturally, you are referring to the *character cue* section of the dialogue block. That's where you must be consistent. There, I would refer to him as JOE/WAYNE or JOE AS WAYNE when he is posing as Wayne.

Please allow me to clarify the term *character cue* so that everyone knows what I am referring to. A dialogue block consists of three possible sections, named below.

```
            CHARACTER CUE
          (parenthetical)
       Dialogue or spoken words or
       speech.
```

In screenplay writing, you should refer to a character in the character cue section by using the exact same name each time. There are some exceptions, and we have just discussed one of those.

There is one other area where you should be consistent, and that is the writing itself. So...keep writing.

IS FORMATTING THE CAUSE OF INSANITY IN SCREENWRITERS?

QUESTION

I attended a major conference and heard so many contradictory "rules" about formatting that my head is spinning. I was told if a reader, agent, director, producer, etc., sees the following things in your script, you will be immediately branded as an amateur regardless of how good your screenplay is. It's driving me insane! Will you please comment on the following seven "rules" that I heard at this major conference? (Signed: "Seriously considering horticulture instead.")

ANSWER

Dear Horticulturalist: I'll be happy to. I will list your seven "rules" in *italics* and comment on each individually.

Rule 1. Some "experts" said CUT TO is no longer used; others said it doesn't matter.

In a way, both experts are right. Although it's okay to use CUT TO, you should use it sparingly, if at all. If you use any editing direction (CUT TO, DISSSOLVE, WIPE, etc.), there should be a **story** reason for it. Don't use it just for style. The bottom line is this: if I see two or three editing directions in your script, I'm not concerned. If I see one after every scene, then you have a problem.

2. Don't put DAY in the scene heading. Is it now considered presumptuous for the lowly writer to tell the auteur whether it's dark or light outside?

I am as surprised as you. The person who said this probably fled afterwards under the cover of night. Go ahead and indicate DAY (or NIGHT) in your scene headings.

There may be situations where you don't need to indicate DAY or NIGHT if it's already obvious. For example, if you've established that we're inside a house during the daytime (INT. JACK'S HOUSE – DAY), and your next scene location is a room inside that house, you may be able to get by without indicating DAY (INT. JACK'S KITCHEN).

3. No periods or dashes after EXT or INT.

There should be a period after EXT and INT, but no dash. Here's what a master scene heading should look like:

```
EXT. HIGHWAY - DAY
```

4. No ANGLES ON or CLOSE UPS. So how do you tell a director that the audience really needs to see the inscription on a gun or something else that requires a close up?

Avoid camera angles and camera directions. If you want a close up of the gun, simply write:

```
The inscription on the gun says, "No
close ups or you're dead."
```

The above description has to be a CLOSE UP. Part of the art of spec writing is learning how to direct the camera without using camera directions.

5. Some "experts" said to use no parentheticals [actor's instructions] at all; others said to use parentheticals only for action, not for emotion. I thought action lines showed action.

You're right; they do. However, small bits of action that accompany dialogue may be written as parentheticals. (I'll provide an example a little later.)

And certainly, the main use of parentheticals is to indicate the subtext (or emotional content) of the speech when that subtext would not otherwise be apparent. For example:

```
                RUPERT
            (lovingly)
        You disgust me.
```

One caveat with parentheticals is to not go overboard with them.

6. No dot, dot, dot.

Wrong. Use the ellipsis (three dots in a row) in dialogue to show continuity of thought. What follows is an example.

```
                JOAN
        I thought you were...

                DR. V
        ... dead?
            (he laughs)
        You were mistaken.
```

And—bingo!—I just wrote an action as a parenthetical.

7. And no beats! So how do I show a pause?

You can use the word "beat," but it is rather pedestrian and unimaginative. Use a better word or phrase that implies the pause you want while commenting on character or story.

Here's an example.

```
                SOL
        But you said --
```

```
              LUNA
      -- I said I'd be back by sunset.
          (holding Sol's gaze)
      And I'm not lying.
```

May I share a few final comments? I understand your frustration about formatting. The confusion out there is one reason I donned my Dr. Format tights in the first place.

Please relax and realize that most industry people are not searching for the slightest error in your script as an excuse to shred it. If you make a few little formatting mistakes, your script will not be trashed, especially if it is a well-written script.

However, if you make many formatting errors or gross errors, then insiders will likely look askance at your script. Therefore, it's in your best interests to strive for a professional presentation.

Also, too many writers see formatting as an arbitrary box that they must dump the content of their writing into. They are missing the important point that formatting is part of the writing itself.

It is my hope that you will learn the tools of your trade, including screenplay formatting, and that you will keep writing.

A FLYING HIPPO

QUESTION
I am writing a script that needs to have a certain person's POV [point of view]. Think along the lines of *The Sixth Sense* where the character sees "things." My question is, whenever

my character sees these "things," should I put:

JOE BLOW'S POV - A flying hippo.

ANSWER
Avoid technical intrusions in a spec script. Try to direct the camera without using camera directions. In this case, just write:

Joe Blow sees a flying hippo.

WHAT THE CAMERA SEES

QUESTION
I'm writing a fictional documentary in the style of *Waiting For Guffman, Bob Roberts, Man Bites Dog*, etc., and I am wondering how to write scenes where the "cameraman" is an actual participant in the scene.

Specifically, let's say the cameraman is interviewing someone, when suddenly an explosion occurs and everyone, including the cameraman, runs in terror.

If I write "Cameraman flees the area like a scared rabbit," that implies that we actually SEE him running, but in reality I want him running with the camera still rolling. What's the best way to do this?

ACTION
There are many ways to handle this situation. Here's just one.

Let's cross-cut between what is happening and what the camera sees. Let's say we're already into the scene, and Nancy Cameraperson is filming teen sensation Rocko Jocko, who is being interviewed. All of a sudden...

A nearby explosion rocks the area.

Pandemonium. People run every direction.

THROUGH NANCY'S CAMERA

Rock Jock's plastic smile withers into a
white mask of horror. He flees.
Suddenly, images of people fly by at
awkward angles. There is no up or down.

BACK TO SCENE

Nancy runs, her camera bouncing awkwardly
from her hand. Debris begins to fall from
the sky.

THROUGH NANCY'S CAMERA

A man trips and falls hard on the
sidewalk. The image blurs from sidewalk
to sky. A black and white plume of smoke
billows into the blue.

A uniformed man falls from somewhere
right on us. Blackness.

BACK TO SCENE

Nancy is on the ground looking up. The
uniformed man has fallen on her and on
the camera. A siren wails. Nancy
struggles to her feet.

And then, keep cutting back and forth until the scene ends.

TELL US A STORY

QUESTION
My story begins in a therapist's office after everything that is going to happen in the screenplay happens. Basically, the entire screenplay is going to be a flashback. The first scene is in the therapist's office and then cuts to the past. And then, in the last scene, we'll cut back to the therapist's office. Should I label this a FLASHBACK?

ANSWER
No. You are using the storyteller device. Open in the therapist's office, and then cut to the past; that is, cut to a new scene heading, followed by a bit of narrative description, followed by a SUPER. The SUPER (short for superimpose) will look something like this.

```
SUPER: "Six Months Earlier"
```

ASPIRING TO DIRECT

QUESTION
I'm looking to use my writing abilities to help launch a directing career. When sending out a query letter (with script), is it appropriate to mention this at all?

ANSWER
No. And don't send your script with your query. The purpose of your query should be to get the agent or producer to request your script. Wait until that agent or producer is in love with your script before pushing your directing skills. At such a time, you will need a "reel" (video or DVD) of footage that you directed, such as a short film.

DOUBLE AGENTS

QUESTION
What if more than one agent requests my script, should I send the script out to both?

ANSWER
You should be so lucky. The answer is "yes." If both end up loving your script, then you will simply make a choice between the two. I had a client with this very "problem." She found a producer who loved her script and he referred her to several agents, whom she interviewed until she found the one she wanted. I wish the same success for you.

A SUPER IDEA

QUESTION
I just want the words "8 months ago" to appear on the screen on top of some images I describe. What is the proper formatting for this? Do I use a SUPER, as follows?

```
EXT. DON'S BAR - EVENING

SUPER: "8 MONTHS AGO."

Al and Doug sit at the counter with empty
shot glasses lining the bar.
```

ANSWER
Yes.

However, you might consider placing the SUPER *after* some narrative description. Sometimes, it works better to establish something visually before superimposing some words. In other words, write this:

```
EXT. DON'S BAR - NIGHT

Al and Doug sit at the counter with empty
shot glasses lining the bar.

SUPER: "EIGHT MONTHS EARLIER."
```

And then write some more narrative description.

You'll notice in the above example that I slightly altered the wording of your SUPER. Both of the above examples are "correct." It's your dramatic choice which you use.

CAN YOU SUPER A SCROLL?

QUESTION
What's the proper format to write superimposed exposition like that at the beginning of *Star Wars*, for example?

ANSWER
You can either use the term SCROLL or SUPER. It's your choice. If you have more than a paragraph to SCROLL or SUPER, then format the paragraphs as you would dialogue; that is, indent by 10 spaces the entire quoted text to be superimposed.

Here's something else to keep in mind. Regardless of whether you superimpose one word or three paragraphs, place the entire superimposition in quotations marks. For example:

```
SUPER:

          "Long ago in a galaxy far away
          there lived an odd little man
          who said his verbs before his
          nouns."
```

IT'S UP TO YOU

QUESTION

I have a technical question about the MONTAGE. I've seen different ways to format a MONTAGE. Is one wrong, or is it a matter of choice? Here are two examples.

```
MONTAGE - ANN'S SPENDING SPREE

-- INT. SAKS -- Ann buys every pair of
shoes she tries on.

-- INT. POTTERY BARN -- Ann buys a set of
cookware and dozens of kitchen gadgets.
```

Or, is this correct:

```
MONTAGE - ANN'S SPENDING SPREE

-- At Saks, Ann buys every pair of shoes
she tries on.

-- At the Pottery Barn, Ann buys a set of
cookware and dozens of kitchen gadgets.
```

ANSWER

It's a matter of choice. You can use either one, and there are other slight variations that also work.

FOLLOW-UP QUESTION

Is the following indentation necessary?

```
-- At the Pottery Barn, Ann buys a set of
   cookware along with every kitchen
   gadget in the store.
```

ANSWER
It's okay to indent like that, but it is not necessary.

MAY I INSERT?

QUESTION
If you use an INSERT or SERIES OF SHOTS [or other special heading], and it will not all fit on the same page, do you simply continue on the next page, or must you start at the top of the next page?

ANSWER
Continue on the next page.

DO I HAVE THE RIGHT APARTMENT?

QUESTION
About scene headings, if the movie starts in an apartment, but the apartment belongs to the main character, do I write:

```
INT. JACK'S APARTMENT - DAY
```

or

```
INT. APARTMENT - DAY
```

since no one knows his name yet?

ANSWER
It's okay to refer to the apartment as JACK'S APARTMENT, since Jack will be introduced in the next paragraph. It's also okay to simply refer to it as an APARTMENT.

NUMBER RULES

QUESTION
From your Dr. Format column, I know that numbers must be written out as words in dialogue, but what about narrative description? For example, if a customer hands a cashier $12.50, would I write it with the Arabic numerals or spell it out in word form as I would in dialogue.

ANSWER
You may use Arabic numerals (just as you do in your question above) when writing narrative description (action).

WHAT COLOR IS YOUR COVER?

QUESTION
What color should a script cover be? Is there a standard color or colors? I have also seen script covers made of linen paper. Is that okay?

ANSWER
Use index stock for your cover. Just go to Kinko's or any other copy shop and ask for 110-pound index stock. Linen paper is unnecessary. The color is irrelevant, although most covers are a light color.

NAME THAT NAME

QUESTION
I am currently working on a military/action script, and my central character is Captain James Lee. In the character cue, should the name be written as CAPTAIN SMITH, SMITH, OR JAMES?

ANSWER
It can be any of the above, depending on the situation. A rule-of-thumb is to choose the name that is most likely to stand out. For example, if all of the characters have military rank and are referred to in the character cue by their rank, you might consider using JAMES or SMITH for this character to make him stand out from the others.

As a very general guideline, use the first name for good guys, and the last name for bad guys. Readers tend to warm up to "first names." Military officers should usually be referred to by their rank—CAPTAIN SMITH.

PROGRESSIVE WRITING

QUESTION
I know that the progressive tense is frowned upon in action description. "Joe runs" is preferred to "Joe is running." But what about in parentheticals? Is there really any difference between the following two examples?

Example #1:

                    MAX
              (whispering)
         Over here.

Example #2:

                    MAX
              (whispers)
         Over here.

It seems to me that, since the parenthetical refers to something that happens at the moment the dialogue is delivered, "whispering" would be just fine. What do you say?

ANSWER
Either works for me. Keep writing.

WRITING UNDERCOVER

QUESTION
When using initials, such as CIA or FBI, in dialogue, what is
the proper format?

ANSWER
If the character says the letters, then use hyphens or periods, as
follows: C-I-A or C.I.A.

If the character uses an acronym that is pronounced like a
word, just write out the acronym in all-CAPS.

Here's an example.

```
                    REPORTER
          The woman from MADD was thought
          to be F.B.I. until officials saw
          her UNICEF badge.
```


MUSICAL CHAIRS

QUESTION
How do you format a transition to a scene where you only
hear music or dialogue before anything visual actually comes
up on the screen?

ANSWER
This is best answered with an example.   First, I'll set up the
situation and then go to a hip-hop tune. You'll hear the tune
before you see anything.

Sam and Selma stare at each other in
silent rapture. He takes her hand.

                    PREACHER (V.O.)
          Do you Sam Bopeep take Selma
          Gillycut as your lawfully wedded
          wife...

INT. CHAPEL - DAY

A small crowd in a small chapel watch the
PREACHER continue.

                    PREACHER
          ... through sickness and health,
          until death do you part?

Sam looks like he's being strangled by
his tie. His eyes dart about.

A high-voltage hip-hop tune plays.

INT./EXT. CAR - DAY

The hip-hop tune plays from the car
radio. Sam's hand turns up the volume.
He's alone in the car.

EXT. CHAPEL - DAY

The car, decorated with "Just married"
paraphernalia on it, screeches away as
the wedding crowd exits the chapel, led
by an angry Selma.

GROUPIES

QUESTION
When a main character with a speaking part is introduced for the first time, his or her name is entered in CAPS. I know this is also the case with minor characters that have one or two lines. However, are groups of characters with no lines entered in CAPS when introduced for the first time in a script?

For example, is this correct?

```
Ten armed guards enter the street, which
is full of busy merchants and customers.
```

ANSWER
Yes.

IF PIGS COULD FLY

QUESTION
Recently, someone told me that after an INSERT, I must come BACK TO SCENE, as shown in Example #1 below.

Example #1

```
Joe picks up the paper.  His eyes widen
as he reads.

INSERT - THE HEADLINE, which reads:
"PIGS FLY."

BACK TO SCENE

A raucous laugh.  He climbs up on the
table and does a little dance.
```

Isn't it already obvious that we go BACK TO SCENE? Would my second example below be okay?

Example #2

```
Joe picks up the paper.  His eyes widen
as he reads the headline:

PIGS FLY.

A raucous laugh.  He climbs up on the
table and does a little dance.
```

ANSWER
If you are going to use the INSERT, bring us BACK TO SCENE, for the sake of clarity. Example #1 is correct.

But you don't necessarily have to use the INSERT. Since the story reason for the INSERT is to draw attention to something, just draw our attention to the headline with a separate paragraph as follows:

```
The headline reads: "PIGS FLY."
```

That's just as clear as the INSERT (Example #1). And it implies a newspaper headline large enough that you would not need to INSERT a separate shot.

Or you could write:

```
Joe's eyes widen when he sees the .
headline.

                    JOE
          Pig's fly?
```

Concerning your Example #2 above, the phrase "PIGS FLY"

looks like it could be mistaken for a scene heading (slug line). That's potentially confusing, so don't use Example #2. Remember to put quotation marks around any words that you want to appear on the movie screen.

FLASHY FLASHBACKS

QUESTION
If there is a flashback to only about a week prior that ends in an event that has been see in the movie before, how would you write it?

ANSWER
A FLASHBACK is a FLASHBACK. You would format this as a FLASHBACK.

FOLLOW UP QUESTION
Here is an example of the original scene that I have in mind:

A man and two women are in a room eating. A third woman enters the room. The third woman says, "Have you no shame, little man?"

That's the original scene. Later, the flashback sequence shows the third woman preparing and getting dressed and ends with her walking into the room, but not saying those words. *But* it is meant to be in the past. In the script, how would you write this so the reader knows it happened in the past without having to compromise what you want the character to say or do?

ANSWER
The short answer is this: the reader will know it happened in the past because it will be labeled as a FLASHBACK. I'm not seeing a reason for not calling it a FLASHBACK. I suppose an alternative would be to use a SUPER, as follows:

SUPER: "One week prior."

The problem with your question is you want to change what happened in the past, which makes no sense. If the third woman spoke certain words in a past scene, then she should speak them in the flashback to that past scene, unless you don't want to show that specific part of the past. Perhaps that is your intent.

Having established that, let's format the flashback from the information you have given me. I'll add some details of my own. Let's call the third woman Vivian and the little man Mort. I think, in this case, that a FLASHBACK MONTAGE would work well.

FLASHBACK MONTAGE - VIVIAN LEARNS THE TRUTH

-- VIVIAN'S BEDROOM -- Vivian puts the finishing touches on her makeup. Her formal outfit is stunning. She picks up her purse and leaves the room.

-- MORT'S DINING ROOM -- Mort, wearing a t-shirt, and two women sit around a table and a KFC bucket.

-- VIVIAN'S CAR -- She drives impatiently, glancing at her watch.

-- MORT'S DINING ROOM -- Mort and the two women laugh together as they eat the chicken. Mort hears a door open and close, and looks like he wants to hide. Vivian walks in; she freezes -- shocked.

END FLASHBACK MONTAGE

We cut right there before she can say, "Have you no shame, Little Man."

The above is not a particularly exciting scene, but it shows you how to handle your problem.

DO YOU SEE WHAT I SEE?

QUESTION
A character in my story is experiencing the after effects of a drug he has mistakenly taken. When writing what he sees and hears, how should I format it? Should I just describe what he sees, or put a slugline of "intoxicated vision" or something before that?

ANSWER
Let's call this guy Slim. If Slim's "intoxicated vision" is a hallucination or a vision of something that is not real or actually happening, then use a scene heading (slug line) similar to this:

```
SLIM'S HALLUCINATION
```

or

```
SLIM'S DRUG-INDUCED VISION
```

and then describe it.

However, if what Slim sees *is* real, but is distorted because of the drugs, then you simply describe what he sees:

```
Slim sees everything in bright colors.
Shapes are distorted.  Sylvia's head
looks like a talking green papaya.
```

HE SAYS, SHE SAYS

QUESTION
If my plot is about a female character disguising herself as a male, do I head her dialogue blocks as JACK or JANE AS JACK or what? Also, in the description, do I refer to this character as he or she?

ANSWER
The character is Jane, so you should refer to her as Jane in the narrative description, and you should use the feminine pronouns "she" and "her" in narrative description. However, in the character cue of your dialogue block, you may refer to your character as JANE AS JACK or JANE/JACK for clarity.

Just so you know, it would be proper to refer to her as JANE in the character cue if you thought the reader would not get confused. Since her true identity is Jane and (assuming) that's established early, then consider referring to her as JANE in the character cue throughout the entire screenplay, even though some characters might call her Jack (in dialogue).

I WRITE THE SONGS

QUESTION
I've just finished a piece of work and there are several musical passages. One includes a character who begins to sing a certain song by a current musical artist. How would you format it?

ANSWER
You probably wouldn't mention a specific song. You are usually better off referring to music generically. For example:

```
Thelma sings a sad Country-Western tune.
```

Please see the question and answer below for the correct format for lyrics. For more on specific songs, see pp. 21-22.

I PEN THE POEMS

QUESTION
My character reads a poem to an audience. How do I format it?

ANSWER
The words of song lyrics and poems are written as dialogue. You could present the lines in verse form, or you could place a slash at the end of each line.

Here's an example of both methods.

Verse form:

```
            DELLA
         (singing)
    Roses are red.
    Violets are blue.
    Sugar is sweet,
    And so are you.
```

With slashes at the end of each line:

```
            DELLA
         (singing)
    Roses are red/Violets
    are blue/Sugar is
    sweet/And so are you.
```

IT'S ALL THE SAME

QUESTION
Is there any difference between using SAME and CONTINUOUS in slug lines? Is one more in fashion than the other?

ANSWER
It depends on whom you ask. For the majority of industry people, the terms are used synonymously.

However, many writers use CONTINUOUS to refer to a scene that comes right after the previous scene without any loss of time, and use SAME to refer to a scene that happens at the same time as the previous scene; in other words, overlapping. To avoid any possible confusion, I suggest you use CONTINUOUS.

What follows are two examples, one using CONTINUOUS and one using SAME.

Example #1:

```
PONCHO wanders down the hall until he
reaches a door.  He turns the door knob.
```

```
EXT. HOUSE - CONTINUOUS
```

```
The door opens and Poncho steps out into
the cold.
```

Example #2

```
INT. SHERMA'S ROOM - NIGHT
```

```
Sherma paces nervously.  She looks at the
clock, then walks to the window
```

```
INT. DEREK'S CAR - SAME
```

Derek drives anxiously through the rain.
He looks at his watch, the peers through
the windshield.

In Example #2, the director has a choice. He or she can place the second scene right after the first, or assume that both scenes happen at the same moment in time and cross-cut the individual beats of each scene: Sherma paces, Derek drives; Sherma looks at the clock, Derek at his watch; and so on.

SASE STANDARDS

QUESTION
When you send a query letter and include an SASE or postcard, do you fill in the return address?

ANSWER
You can, but you don't need to. However, make sure you write the name of the company somewhere on that SASE (self-addressed stamped envelope). You don't want to receive mail and not know who it came from. Be sure to place your own address on the SASE or postcard. And don't forget the stamp.

Some writers state in their queries that they will call the producer or agent. In that case, an SASE is not needed. It's not a bad approach since, as a general rule, good news comes on the phone and bad news through the mail.

CAPPING CHARACTERS

QUESTION
I was told by someone that I should only place in all-CAPS the names of characters that have speaking parts. Therefore, the following example would be incorrect:

```
EMMY MAE pushes past a group of STUNNED
ONLOOKERS as she makes her way to the
podium.
```

Should I only CAP the name of the individual characters that have names, or is it okay to CAP the groups of people themselves (in this case, STUNNED ONLOOKERS).

ANSWER
When a character with a name (whether or not he has a speaking part) first physically appears in the screenplay, you should place that character's name in all-CAPS that one time. You do not need to CAP the names of groups of people.

If you have an individual character that does not have a name, but who is identified by function or looks, I recommend that you place that character's name in all-CAPS the moment she first physically appears in the screenplay (whether or not she has a speaking part). For example, you could write COCKY COP or SLICK SALESLADY when those two characters appear for the first time in the script.

Let's return to your example and format it in accordance with my recommendations. I am assuming that all of these people are appearing in this screenplay for the first time.

```
EMMY MAE pushes past a group of stunned
onlookers as she makes her way to the
podium.
```

```
A SKINNY SECURITY GUARD moves towards
Emma Mae.
```

CAPPING ACTION

QUESTION
I'm trying to figure out if it's best to put actions within "action" in CAPS. Here's a quick example:

```
Duke WAVES to Lassie as he drives off.
```

ANSWER
Don't place actions in all-CAPS. CAPS are hard to read, and the reader might think you are trying to indicate a sound.

Since the primary purpose of narrative description is to describe action, you do not need any emphasis. I like the fact that your example focuses on a verb. If you use specific, concrete action verbs in your description, you'll likely catch the reader's attention.

UNCOORDINATED

QUESTION
Is the following correct? It's the only way I can figure out how to format it.

```
INT. COURTHOUSE - DAY

The judge looks doubtful.

                    JUDGE
          I need to know more about
          the incident.
```

<pre>
                    PROSECUTOR (V.O.)
           Well, your honor, according
           to the proprietor, the
           defendant blah, blah, blah....
</pre>

SERIES OF COORDINATED SHOTS TO (V.O.)
ABOVE

-- Night life along the beach [to set
tone].

-- Inside building, lots of noise, music,
smoke....

-- At other end of the building,
patrons....

-- A fight breaks out and bouncers
pounce....

BACK TO PRESENT COURT SCENE

<pre>
                       JUDGE
           Good Lord! Anything else?
</pre>

ANSWER
I realize that the above is purposely brief to save space. Naturally, you would want your descriptions of shots to be more specific and visually clear. And, of course, you would write out every word the prosecutor says that you want the audience to hear. Having noted that, let's discuss your problem.

The above is poor format. If you are going to have the prosecutor speak while we see a flashback of visual images, then you should write in that fashion. Here's a partial revision to illustrate what I mean.

```
                    PROSECUTOR (V.O.)
          Well, your honor, according
          to the proprietor...
```

EXT. BOARDWALK - NIGHT - FLASHBACK

The defendant runs by a building.

```
                    PROSECUTOR (V.O.)
          ...he saw the defendant
          jogging...
```

He notices smoke pouring out of a window.

And then you would continue the narration over the visual description.

The idea is to describe what we will visually see on the movie screen and hear on the soundtrack. At the end of this scene, you could write:

BACK TO COURTROOM

There is a potential problem in proceeding in the above manner. As a general rule, the narration should not repeat what the audience is already seeing on the silver screen. That's repetitive. Perhaps a more effective approach to this scene would be to let the prosecutor begin his explanation, and then cut to the boardwalk along the beach and show us what happened without any voice over narration.

WHERE TO LOCATE THE LOCATION

QUESTION
I'm trying to write a scene where the end of the scene is part of another location.

For example, Jim squats in his neighbor's yard to defecate, and then I cut to a close up of chocolate yogurt being dispensed at another location. The question is, should I keep the shock suspense in the read by formatting the cut as follows:

```
EXT. NEIGHBOR'S HOUSE - DAY

Jim pulls down his drawers and squats
over his neighbor's lawn.

CLOSE UP: A swirl of chocolate drops.

                              CUT TO:

INT. ICE CREAM PARLOR - DAY

The ice cream man hands a child a bowl of
chocolate yogurt.
```

ANSWER
First of all, delete your reference to CLOSE UP. The camera direction is unnecessary because your description of "a swirl of chocolate" implies a CLOSE UP.

Since the chocolate swirl of yogurt drops at the ice cream parlor and not on the lawn, the description should appear under the scene heading (slug line) for the ICE CREAM PARLOR. Thus, the following would be correct:

```
EXT. NEIGHBOR'S HOUSE - DAY

Jim marches onto the new-mown lawn and
stops.  He glares at his neighbor's front
window, pulls down his drawers, and
squats.

                              CUT TO:
```

```
INT. ICE CREAM PARLOR - DAY

A swirl of chocolate drops.

The ice cream man hands a child a bowl of
chocolate yogurt.
```

I'd like to make two comments regarding the above revision. First, notice that I changed the narrative description a little to add a little drama and characterization to the scene.

Second, I used the "CUT TO." Faithful readers know that I recommend excluding editing directions (such as the CUT TO) from spec scripts. Certainly, you don't need the "CUT TO" in the above revision; it would be "correct" without it. The reason I kept it is to drawn attention to the visual gag. Assuming there are no other (or very few) editing directions in the script, the reader's eye will be drawn to this one.

SINGING THE BLUES

QUESTION
What is the industry-accepted format for writing song lyrics into a character's dialogue? My script concerns a song writer, and I'm uncertain as to what formatting technique I use to write her song numbers into the script. I can't find the answer anywhere.

ANSWER
The reason you don't see much information on this "formatting technique" is because it is not generally used in spec scripts.

It sounds like your character writes songs and so the songs are an important part of the story. But in so doing, you're asking the eventual producer to either accept the music you have already written or to find someone to write music to your lyrics. So not only does the producer have to love your story, he or she has to love the lyrics and the music as well.

Soundtrack movies are almost always developed at a production company or studio. The rights to the music are secured during or before the development process. Musicals are usually plays before they are movies; in such cases, the rights to the original play are purchased before the screenplay is written. Seldom are musicals and music-based movies purchased as spec scripts.

If the songs you want to include in your story are written by existing artists, then you shouldn't write in their lyrics unless you own or control the rights to their songs, nor should you mention specific songs in your spec script. (See pages 21-22.)

These are all reasons it is generally a good idea to avoid music altogether in a spec script and just tell a good story. Coincidentally, I recently wrote a script about a rock star. There are obvious places for music in my script, but I never mention specific songs, nor do I write out any lyrics. That can be done later, after the script is sold.

Now that I've laid all the negatives down, let me say that it is possible that a producer will love your script, music, and lyrics just the way they are. In such a case, the music may help cinch the deal. It only takes one person to love your story.

Finally, here's the answer to your question.

When you write the lyrics of a song, you should write them as dialogue since they are sung by a character. You can write them in stanza form just like a poem. For examples, see page 164.

LOCATION HIERARCHY

QUESTION
I hope you may be able to settle a minor disagreement between a colleague and I regarding the correct format for master scene headings (slug lines). When I write a new location without a preceding establishing shot, I usually start with the specific room, or area in which the action takes place, and then move outwards. For example:

```
INT. LOBBY, FOUR SEASONS HOTEL, LOS
ANGELES - NIGHT
```

In my mind, this offers the most clarity as the first image the reader will conjure up is of a lobby in a swanky hotel, which happens to be in Los Angeles. My colleague, however, believes that the information should be presented in the reverse manner, as follows:

```
INT. LOS ANGELES, FOUR SEASONS HOTEL,
LOBBY - NIGHT
```

So which is correct?

ANSWER
Your colleague is more correct than you are. You should start with the larger location and work down to the smaller location. The scene heading would actually look more like this:

```
INT. LOS ANGELES - FOUR SEASON HOTEL -
LOBBY - NIGHT
```

However, that would not look right because a shot of Los Angeles would have to be an exterior shot, not an interior shot. In this case, I suggest you establish Los Angeles first, as follows:

```
EXT. LOS ANGELES - NIGHT

The city is alive with pedestrians and
traffic.  In the distance sits the Four
Seasons Hotel.

INT. FOUR SEASONS HOTEL - LOBBY - SAME
```

That communicates to the reader that we open with Los Angeles and then move towards the hotel.

Another approach is to open with an exterior of the hotel, and then cut to the lobby. In that case, you could communicate that the hotel is in Los Angeles via a sign on the wall or through dialogue.

IS PAGE 1 REALLY PAGE 1?

QUESTION
If you use a quote to open the script on the page preceding FADE IN, is that page considered page 1, or is the next page beginning with FADE IN still considered the first page?

ANSWER
The page beginning with FADE IN is always page 1.

As a suggestion, don't place a quote on a separate page between the title page and page 1. If that quote is important, and if you want the audience to see it on the movie screen, then it should appear on page 1. Thus, page 1 would look something like this:

```
BLACK SCREEN

SUPER: "Two can live as cheaply as one,
but only half as long."
```

```
FADE IN:

A piggy bank.
```

In terms of how the first few pages your script should look, follow this protocol: Your cover page is first and should consist of blank card stock, any color. It should be followed by your title page. Your title page should be followed by page 1 of your script.

Page 1 should not have a page number typed on it; but page two, and all pages thereafter, will have page numbers appearing in the upper right corner.

DIRECTING THE FOCUS

QUESTION
What should I do in the situation where there are two sets of people talking, and I want the audience to overhear one set while the main focus is on the other?

ANSWER
I think you want something like this.

```
INT. RESTAURANT - NIGHT

Mustafa and Jane sit down at a table.  A
waiter hands them menus.

In a booth behind them, across the aisle,
Fatty and Slim plan.  Mustafa and Jane
cannot hear them.

                    SLIM
          Wait 'til they leave.
```

Slim angrily eyes Mustafa and Jane, who
study their menus.

> FATTY (O.S.)
> I'll follow them out to
> their car.

> SLIM (O.S.)
> They'll get what they deserve
> for not formatting their
> script correctly.

Mustafa lifts a feature script from his
briefcase and places it on the table.

> FATTY (O.S.)
> (incredulously)
> Don't they read Dr. Format's
> column?

In the above scene, the focus is on Mustafa and Jane. As you
can see, most of the dialogue between Fatty and Slim is
spoken off screen (O.S.). A different approach would be to
show Mustafa and Jane overhearing the conversation between
Fatty and Slim.

ACTION BREAKS

QUESTION
When should I break to another paragraph when describing the
action in a screenplay?

ANSWER
A very general rule-of-thumb is one paragraph per image or
beat of action. The following segment presents four beats;
thus, four paragraphs.

Fatty opens his trench coat to reveal a
chain saw.

At the sound of the chain saw starting,
Mustafa and Jane back up against their
car. Mustafa shields them with their
screenplay.

Fatty saws the screenplay in half, turns
off the chain saw, and saunters away.

Mustafa and Jane stare dumbfounded at
their shredded screenplay.

LET ME UNDERSCORE THIS POINT

QUESTION
What's the best way for me to stress a word of dialogue? By
italicizing it, bolding it, or placing it in all-CAPS?

ANSWER
None of the above. If you must emphasize a word or phrase,
underscore it.

A NUMBERS GAME

QUESTION
Could you please tell me if it's necessary to spell out the
following numbers within the dialogue portion of my script?

-- dollar amounts
-- years
-- proper names, when the number is part of the name.

ANSWER

In dialogue, all numbers should be written out as words except for years and proper names. The following is correct:

```
              JAN
    In 1999, I paid three thousand
    dollars for a twenty-five pound
    full-scale replica of R2-D2.
```

In addition, don't abbreviate words you can spell out, such as Dr. (for Doctor) or CA (for California). This general guideline about numbers and abbreviations *only* applies to character speeches (dialogue) and not to the character name above the speech or to narrative description.

DIALOGUE IN MONTAGE

QUESTION

I've got a MONTAGE of shots that shows the passage of time. It also requires a VOICE OVER conversation. Should all the MONTAGE shot descriptions be listed first, followed by the entire V.O. dialogue? Or should the dialogue be interspersed between the shot descriptions.

ANSWER

Interspersed. Insert the dialogue at the point in the action that the audience would hear it or should hear it for dramatic or comedic effect. What follows is an example.

```
MONTAGE - LARRY'S DREAM

-- Larry, wearing an orange cape, races
into a building.  He is chased by a mob
firing weapons at him.
```

> > LARRY (V.O.)
> > I knew I was powerful...

-- Larry bounds up the stairs.

> > LARRY (V.O.)
> > ...but I wasn't sure I could
> > fly.

-- Larry bursts through a rooftop door, races to the edge, hesitates, and jumps off. He falls like a rock.

> > LARRY (V.O.)
> > What do you think it means, Doc?

INT. PSYCHIATRIST'S OFFICE

Larry lies on a couch. Nearby, the psychiatrist looks stumped.

> > PSYCHIATRIST
> > Did you land on your head?

THE RIGHT LEADING LADY

QUESTION
If I have written a screenplay with a specific actress in mind for the lead, and that actress is an executive for her own production company, should I notate that the lead was written for her when I query her company?

ANSWER
First, I will answer your question, and then I will give you a warning.

Yes, indicate as much in your query letter or other correspondence (but not in the screenplay). Let them know it was written for her.

Now the warning: there is a danger in writing anything for any actor. You take a chance of creating a character that comes across as derivative or flat. The last thing you want is for the reader of your script to say, "I've seen this character in other movies." Your character should be original and fresh. It's okay to have that right leading lady in your mind as long as you keep the above warning in your mind at the same time.

THE END

QUESTION
At the end of a script do you recommend THE END and then FADE OUT, or is it just FADE OUT?

ANSWER
It's your choice. However, if you write both, the FADE OUT should come before THE END.

                                        FADE OUT.

                       THE END

SLUGGING IT OUT

QUESTION
In my last screenplay, some of the action scenes take place in stairways because the story is set in a somewhat confined place. Is it possible to use a separate slug line when a character walks down a flight of stairs, or should I write it as part of the narrative?

ANSWER
If you have a scene that takes place on a flight of stairs, then you could use the following scene heading (slug line):

INT. FLIGHT OF STAIRS

If the stairs are part of a larger scene where the master location is a house, use the following as your master scene heading:

INT. HOUSE - DAY

And then use the following secondary heading (for the secondary location):

AT THE STAIRWAY

or

ON THE STAIRS

Here's another example:

Juanita races up

THE STAIRS

but stops halfway. She sees a man with a mask charging towards her.

And you would let the scene play out right there AT THE STAIRS.

INSERTION ORDER

QUESTION
Must I always use an INSERT for a close-up? For example,

do I have to use the INSERT for the following:

```
INSERT - A COFFEE MUG, which reads:

        "To protect and serve."

BACK TO SCENE
```

ANSWER
Although the above is perfectly correct and perfectly okay to use, you are free to use the following method, which is also correct:

```
A coffee mug reads, "To protect and
serve."
```

When faced with a choice like this, I usually opt for the simplest version as long as it is clear. In this case, it is.

GETTING THE TREATMENT

QUESTION
I understand what the treatment is and what it is used for, but I'm getting mixed information about length. You once stated that most treatments are about three to seven pages, but there are some articles online that state that a treatment could be twenty-five or more pages. To add to my confusion, I came across treatments for *Aliens* and *Terminator* that were around forty-five pages in length. Could you please clarify?

ANSWER
Your treatment should be usually about 3-7 pages when it is used to sell your project; that is, when it is used to entice people to ask for your screenplay. However, some selling treatments can be as long as 10-14 pages. My rule-of-thumb

is to use as few pages as necessary to sell the material since Hollywood types don't like to read more than they have to.

Usually, your first contact with someone in the business is through a written query letter or an oral pitch. If the query or pitch does its job, then the agent, producer, or executive will likely request a copy of the script, but she could ask for a treatment first or for both the script and a treatment or a one-sheet (one page synopsis). If a treatment is requested, it's easy to ask the requesting party what she is looking for in terms of length.

Occasionally, a producer may request that a treatment or synopsis be included with a query. In such rare cases, the page length will be implied or stated.

As you can see, with the above two scenarios, it's easy to determine about how many pages the agent or producer is looking for. Keep in mind that a treatment can be as long or short as the producer or agent who requests it wants it to be.

If you are an established writer or have some kind of track record, you might be able to sell a treatment or use it to get a deal to write the eventual script. In those cases, use as few pages as necessary to adequately "treat" the story. That will usually be 3-7 pages, but it can be longer. A friend of mine recently wrote two successful treatments; one was three pages in length, and the other was ten pages. He told me the first story needed fewer pages than the second to sell.

In the case of a *development deal* (where a producer hires you to write a script from scratch), you might be asked to write a 45-50 page treatment before writing the first draft of the screenplay. In your question, you referred to two 45-page treatments, one for *Aliens* and the other for *Terminator*; those projects were developed.

I mentioned earlier the term *synopsis.* Although a synopsis can be used as another term for *treatment,* a synopsis usually refers to a 1-3 page story summary. Depending on who is asking for it, it could be written to inform (as with a *coverage*) or to sell.

CAPS, ITALICS, DASHES AND ELLIPSES

QUESTION
When do I use a dash or an ellipsis in dialogue? Also, are there guidelines for emphasizing a word or phrase in a speech? For example, do I use italics or all-CAPS to emphasize that word or phrase?

ANSWER
As a general guideline for dialogue, do not place any words in all-CAPS or *italics.* If you must emphasize a word or phrase of dialogue, underscore it. Also, never use more than one exclamation point at the end of a sentence, and use exclamation points sparingly. Your dialogue should not look like a want ad!!!!

If a character interrupts or is interrupted, use a dash to show that interruption. To show continuity of thought, use an ellipsis. What follows is an example Mary interrupting John and then John continuing Mary's sentence.

JOHN

```
What I want --
```

MARY

```
-- Don't tell me what you...
ah...
```

JOHN

```
... want?
```

In dialogue punctuation, you can get away with just about anything; often, dashes and ellipses are used interchangeably. However, if you use reserve certain marks for specific purposes, you enhance your ability to communicate your story. Finally, only use dashes and ellipses when necessary. Most often, you should use commas and periods.

GOING CAPS CRAZY

QUESTION
[In narrative description] should my characters' names ALWAYS appear in all-CAPS, or only at first mention?

ANSWER
Place the character's name in all-CAPS only when he or she first physically appears in the screenplay. That means you don't need to place the name in all-CAPS when the person is mentioned in dialogue, nor do you need to place the name in all-CAPS more than just that one time when she first physically appears.

Keep in mind that all-CAPS are hard to read, so don't go CAPS crazy. Character first appearances and rare technical/camera directions are the only instances where all-CAPS must be used in narrative description. You may place SOUNDS in all-CAPS if you wish, but do not place props or objects in all-CAPS.

FORMATTING OF WRYLIES

QUESTION
Am I correct that the following parenthetical is incorrectly formatted?

```
                    DOLLY
        I'm Dolly Duncan.   (Twirling her
        golden baton.)   My father owns HG
        Hummers.
```

ANSWER
You're right that it's wrong. Wrylies should not be capitalized, and the period is unnecessary. Also, wrylies should be given their own place in the dialogue block. The following is correct:

```
                    DOLLY
        I'm Dolly Duncan.
             (twirling her golden
              baton)
        My daddy owns HG Hummers.
```

IT DEPENDS ON YOUR POINT-OF-VIEW

QUESTION
How to I write a scene that shows what my character Bob sees through a pair of binoculars.

ANSWER
You appear to be describing a point-of-view (POV) shot through binoculars. What follows is one of many ways to handle the situation in a spec script.

```
INT. HOTEL ROOM - DAY

Bob sits next to his hotel window and
picks up his binoculars.

THROUGH THE BINOCULARS

Bob sees a crowded corner newsstand,
```

where hundreds of people purchase copies
of <u>Script</u> magazine.

BACK TO SCENE

Bob drops the binoculars and dashes out
of the room.

The notation "BACK TO SCENE" can be replaced with
"BACK TO HOTEL ROOM" if you prefer. The following
version is also correct and perhaps more technically sound:

INT. HOTEL ROOM - DAY

Bob sits next to his hotel window and
picks up his binoculars.

EXT. CORNER NEWSTAND - THROUGH THE
BINOCULARS

Hundreds of people purchase copies of
<u>Script</u> magazine.

INT. HOTEL ROOM

Bob drops the binoculars and dashes out
of the room.

The following third version is correct, but I don't think it flows
quite as well as the first two:

INT. HOTEL ROOM - DAY

Bob sits next to his hotel window and
picks up his binoculars.

THROUGH THE BINOCULARS

```
EXT. CORNER NEWSTAND

Hundreds of people purchase copies of
Script magazine.

INT. HOTEL ROOM

Bob drops the binoculars and dashes out
of the room.
```

CAR SHOTS

QUESTION
Should the slug line [scene heading] for a scene showing a man inside a car that is outdoors say INT or EXT?

ANSWER
It depends.

First, let's clearly understand what INT. and EXT. mean. The references (INT. and EXT.) are to the camera location. INT. CAR means the camera is inside the car with the man. EXT. CAR means the camera is outside the car looking through the windshield or the car windows at the man. For that reason, many writers write something like this:

```
INT./EXT. CAR - DAY
```

That means that the camera can be inside or outside the car, giving the option to the director.

It also makes it easier for you, the writer; you won't have to CUT back and forth between interior (INT.) and exterior (EXT.) shots.

PLAYBACK

QUESTION
How to you handle showing a conversation being heard when a character plays back an audio recording.

ANSWER
The dialogue on a taped recording is *voiced over* (**V.O.**); thus, it would be formatted as follows.

```
Bond flicks "Play" on his micro cassette
and listens.

                    FIONA (V.O.)
          Oh, James.  James.  Oh,
          James.
```

This principle applies to voices heard through the telephone, radio, or similar device, or any dialogue that is voiced over; meaning, any dialogue that is not spoken at the scene location.

By comparison, dialogue spoken by a character who is at the camera location, but who is not on screen (in the camera's view), is called *off screen* dialogue (**O.S.**).

CAMERA DIRECTIONS

QUESTION
You preach that screenwriters should direct the camera without using camera directions. How would I do that for an opening scene where the camera pans the inside of a room, indicating various objects that help establish the character?

ANSWER
One way is to have a character walk through the room and

look at each object.   Another way is to describe the objects one by one, as follows:

```
INT. JUDD'S ROOM - DAY

The door is painted purple in contrast to
the bright green walls littered with
posters of science stars -- Einsten,
Hawking, Newton.

Astrology charts and books sit on an old
desk.  Behind the desk is a large book
case overflowing with books.
```

...And so on.   Notice that we pan from the door to the walls to the desk to behind the desk.

CAMERA ANGLES

QUESTION
How do you handle changing the camera angle in a scene where doing so is important to the drama of the scene?

I need to do this in a scene where a man is in his office talking on the phone, a scene the audience has seen a couple of times before, but always with the camera showing the man.   But now I want the camera to show, from behind the man, what's out the window that the man was looking at and wasn't visible to the audience in the previous scenes.

ANSWER
First, let's establish the set-up scene.

```
INT. HIGH RISE OFFICE - DAY

John, phone to ear, laughs heartily.  He
```

suddenly stops, his expression a mask of
terror. He drops the phone and steps
back.

Now let's write the scene with the new camera angle.

INT. HIGH RISE OFFICE - DAY - FLASHBACK

John's back shakes as he laughs on the
phone.

Suddenly, at the window in front of him
appears a window washer...with a gun.

John drops the phone and steps back.

There's probably a hundred ways to write the above. And
there may be rare situations where you will use a camera
direction or a camera angle or a technical direction in a spec
screenplay. But first explore more creative ways, and then, if
you feel you must use camera directions, do so very sparingly.

READERS AND THE CAMERA

QUESTION
If you could only name one thing that a reader [story analyst]
wants, what would it be?

ANSWER
May I name more than one? I'll be brief.

Readers want a wonderful story and original characters. And
readers want a screenplay that is clear and easy to read. That's
one reason for the exclusion of camera directions and other
technical intrusions. Words and phrases in all-CAPS are more
difficult to read, and slow down the reading process.

Your narrative should describe visual images and sounds in clear, specific terms. It is more important to be clear than to be literary, and more effective to be readable than technical. Strive for short paragraphs; no paragraph should be longer than four lines.

HEADLINE HEADINGS

QUESTION
I have no idea how to insert various news headlines. There are four headlines I want to use and I just don't know how to go about it.

ANSWER
If there were just one headline, you would use the INSERT heading and indent the headline as you would dialogue.

```
INSERT - NEWS HEADLINE, which reads:

          "Red Sox Win!"

BACK TO SCENE
```

The INSERT heading is normally used for one insertion, although the following would work. (I'm using actual headlines that have appeared in newspapers.)

```
INSERT - NEWSPAPERS

They drop on a table in succession with
the following headlines:

          "Milk Drinkers Turn to Powder"

          "New Housing for Elderly Not
          yet Dead"
```

```
          "Man Fatally Slain"

          "Convict Evades Noose; Jury Hung"

BACK TO SCENE
```

Options abound, but here's one last solution.

```
MONTAGE - NEWS HEADLINES

-- "Jill Escribe Wins Oscar!"

-- "Best Screenplay Goes to Newcomer!"

-- "Jill Escribe Signs 4-Picture Deal"

-- "Praise for Script Magazine and Dr.
Format"
```

THE MESSAGE IS IN THE TEXT

QUESTION
How would I format an e-mail conversation between two people?

ANSWER
My answer applies to text messaging, instant messaging, emailing, and the like. The general principle is you should indent any written dialogue as you would oral dialogue.

What follows assumes the entire scene is handled at one location, Burt's room. Also, instead of using BURT as a secondary scene heading (as I do below), I could write BACK TO SCENE or BACK TO BURT. Finally, the following is just one of many ways to handle the situation.

Burt types on his laptop.

ON BURT'S LAPTOP SCREEN

> "Jan, come with me to
> Showcase."

BURT

stands up and paces around his desk until
he hears a little PING. He scrambles to
his laptop.

ON BURT'S LAPTOP SCREEN

Jan's words appear:

> "Was gonna break it off, but
> Since you mention Showcase,
> okay."

BURT

screams for joy, then types with a
flourish.

ON BURT'S LAPTOP SCREEN

> "Keep writing."

TWO LOCATIONS ARE BETTER THAN ONE

QUESTION
I've seen slug lines containing more than one location. What
gives? Also, can character names be used as slug lines?

ANSWER
In some cases, you may want to include both a master location and a secondary location in the same scene heading, as follows:

```
INT. SMITH HOME - KITCHEN - DAY
```

Naturally, there can be a number of other secondary locations at the Smith home; for example, the living room, a bedroom, a hallway, the stairs, and so on.

Sometimes a person's name can be used as a secondary scene heading, as follows.

```
JASON

loads his gun.
```

If you do this, keep in mind that the camera is on that person until another scene heading indicates we are at a different location. Thus, in the above example, you could not describe the bad guys entering the room without first writing a new scene heading.

TWO LOCATIONS AT ONCE

QUESTION
If opening a scene with two people simultaneously preparing for work, but in two different locations, is there a need to say CUT TO with each cut?

ANSWER
No. You do not need to use CUT TO or any other editing direction (transition) in a spec script.

It's perfectly okay to present a series of scenes, each scene beginning with a scene heading (slug line). However, there might be a more effective method.

If your two characters are each staying in one location, you could use the INTERCUT as follows:

```
INTERCUT - TARA'S BEDROOM/MEL'S BEDROOM

Tara gazes at her mirror; she smiles
confidently.

Mel gazes at his mirror; he looks
worried.
```

And so on.

If your two characters are going to be in several locations, you might consider a MONTAGE, as follows:

```
MONTAGE - TARA AND MEL PREPARE FOR WORK

-- IN MEL'S BEDROOM -- Mel frantically
knots his tie.

-- IN TARA'S BEDROOM -- Tara brushes her
hair with a creative flair.

-- IN MEL'S CAR -- Mel jabbers on his
cell MOS.
```

And so on.

(By the way, MOS means "without sound.")

THREE LOCATIONS AT ONCE

QUESTION
How would you write a phone conversation where the screen is split in half or in thirds?

ANSWER
I suggest you establish the three characters at the three locations first, and then write:

SCREEN SPLITS IN THIRDS

Then just write your dialogue and description much like we did in the MONTAGE in the earlier section ("Two Locations at Once"). If you want to create your split gradually, then write something like the following:

INT. LARRY'S JALOPY - DAY

Larry punches numbers on his cell phone.

SPLIT SCREEN - LARRY'S JALOPY/MOE'S PARLOR

Moe, dressed to the nines, picks up the phone.

                    MOE
          Let me conference Curly.

SCREEN SPLITS IN THIRDS - JALOPY/PARLOR/ CURLY'S BATHROOM

A singing Curly sits in a tub full of bubble bath. He reaches for his ringing phone.

You don't need to get more technical than that. If you're going to do something like a SPLIT SCREEN, make sure you have a compelling dramatic or comedic reason for doing so.

TV TRANSITION

QUESTION
What is the correct way to describe the situation where videotaped footage is shown on a monitor in a television studio before cutting to an interviewer with an interviewee who discuss what was in the video footage just shown?

ANSWER
What you describe could be visualized in a number of ways. That means there are a variety of ways to approach the situation. In any case, the formatting problem is really about how to make the transition from the monitor to the interviewer. Here is what I see.

```
EXT. BURNING HOUSE - DAY

The house is completely engulfed.
Firefighters battle the blaze.

INT. TV STUDIO - DAY

Video of the same burning house plays on
a TV monitor.

Below on an interview couch sit Zeraldo
and a uniformed Fire Captain who watch
the TV monitor.

Zeraldo turns his head towards the studio
cameras.
```

If Zeraldo and the Fire Captain are appearing in the screenplay for the first time, then their names above would appear in all-CAPS.

If Zeraldo and the Fire Captain are watching a live broadcast of the burning building from the TV studio, I would show that by using the term SAME (meaning "at the same time"), as follows.

```
INT. TV STUDIO - SAME
```

I would then adjust the description accordingly.

SPEED DATING

QUESTION
Please help with a scene that involves my character Melanie, sitting at a table, who talks with three men in sequence during a speed dating session. Here is what I have written so far.

```
INT. BLUES BAR - NIGHT

During the whole sequence the camera
stays on the men's face, like an
interrogation/interview.

A nervous MAN sits at Table 4.

                    MAN #1
          Samantha?

                    MELANIE
          Excuse me?
```

                        MAN #1
          You're not Samantha? Oh, I see
          your badge now. Sorry. Then I
          cannot talk. I'm only here for
          Samantha.

                        MELANIE
          What?

The dialogue continues until....

                        MAN #1
            Three minutes! Times up.

                                      CUT TO:

A MAN older than Man #1 sits at Table 4.

And so on.

ANSWER
Let's avoid the editing direction (CUT TO) and write this using one master scene heading along with three secondary headings.

Also, to keep the camera on the three men, we'll simply put Melanie off screen (O.S.). Also, let's give each man a bit more personality and provide some description of the master location.

INT. BLUES BAR - NIGHT

Dark and smoky. Sultry music. Ten
couples sit at ten tables.

AT TABLE 4

```
sits TWITCHY MAN fumbling with a
cigarette.

                    TWITCHY MAN
          Samantha?

                    MELANIE (O.S.)
          Excuse me?

                    TWITHY MAN
          You're not Samantha?  Oh, I see
          your badge now.  Sorry.  Then I
          cannot talk.  I'm only here for
          Samantha.

                    MELANIE (O.S.)
          What?
```

The dialogue continues until....

```
                    TWITCHY MAN
          Three minutes!  Time's up.

MOMENTS LATER

AGED HIPPIE sits at the same table.
```

And so on, until we've seen all three men. The above, of course, is not the only way to handle the situation, but it is one way.

WRESTLING WITH ACTION DESCRIPTIONS

QUESTION
I'm writing a screenplay about the world of professional wrestling, and I'm wondering how specific I have to be in

wrestling and fight scenes. Do I need to write them out move by move, or is that considered amateurish? Is it enough to give a general description and maybe specify only key moves?

ANSWER

I think you have the right idea in that last question. You don't usually need to describe every specific action, but you need to describe enough of the action that the reader can "see" what is happening. Thus, you will use specific language and describe specific details, but you will not usually need to describe every detail.

In dramatic moments, such as the end of the fight, you might want to describe all of those last specific moves. To be honest, there's an element of subjectivity here, and you must decide how much description is enough for your particular screenplay.

In reading the wonderful sword fight scene in William Goldman's *The Princess Bride,* you'll notice that many specific actions are described, and that there are sections of summary descriptions.

What follows is the description of specific moves:

Inigo dives from the stairs to a moss-covered bar suspended over the archway. He swings out, lands, and scrambles to his sword.

The Man in Black casually tosses his sword to the landing where it sticks perfectly.

Then, the Man in Black copies Inigo. Not copies exactly, improves. He dives for the bar, swings completely over it like a

```
circus performer and dismounts with a 9.7
backflip.
```

Then, a little later, we have a summary description that describes specific details:

```
Inigo, moving like lightning, thrusts
forward, slashes, darts back, all in
almost a single movement and...
```

```
The Man in Black dodges, blocks, and
again thrusts forward, faster than ever
before, and again he slashes.
```

Notice the use of action verbs.

Earlier in the scene, the following summary description appears:

```
And in a frenzy, the Man in Black makes
every feint, tries every thrust, lets go
with all he has left. But he fails.
Everything fails. He tries one or two
final desperate moves but they are
nothing.
```

In the above example, we don't see any specific moves, but we get a good sense of what is happening, especially in the context of the action that has preceded this moment (which I have not provided).

The bottom line is to help the reader visualize the action, and to keep the reader excited, enthralled, and intrigued without confusing her.

FORMATTING SOFTWARE

QUESTION
What is your recommendation for formatting software?

ANSWER
I like Movie Magic Screenwriter and Final Draft. Both are worthwhile software programs for the spec writer. For a detailed comparison of the two, visit my web site at keepwriting.com and click on "*Muse*Letter." You'll easily spot the article.

MUST FORMATTING BE PERFECT?

QUESTION
Is it true that if you violate screenplay format in any tiny way, you're immediately rejected?

ANSWER
No.

If you've written a riveting story, but there are a few minor errors in formatting, the script is not going to be tossed into the can, in most cases. The problem comes when your errors in formatting become confusing or distracting to the reader. When a writer pays insufficient attention to formatting conventions or uses his own inimitable formatting style, the resulting script is usually both confusing and distracting.

Your goal, therefore, is to strive for correct format and be consistent in how you apply formatting tools, but not to obsess over it to the point that you buy a hand gun. Perfection is not the goal; excellence is.

FORMATTING FOR WRITER/PRODUCERS

QUESTION
If am going to produce my screenplay myself, do I need to correctly format it?

ANSWER
You may not need to be as particular, but you will still need to communicate what you want to the director, crew and cast in a language they understand. You will still need a script that can be "broken down."

TO FORMAT OR NOT TO FORMAT....

QUESTION
Why must a script be formatted, if the point is to tell a good story?

ANSWER
The short answer is because you want to sell your *script*. It's possible to sell your story in treatment form, but it will be for a lot less money.

As a developing writer, it's normal to view formatting conventions as a kind of an arbitrary rigid box that you must force the content of your story into, but that's missing the point. It's time to re-frame.

Formatting is the language of screenplays. It's a *flexible* communication guide for expressing your story in a way that other professional collaborators (producers, directors, cinematographers, readers, agents, and others) can clearly understand. In reality, formatting guidelines truly are a friend.

Good luck and keep writing.

THE NEW SPEC STYLE
—updated—

This article was originally published by
The Hollywood Scriptwriter

There has been a lot of talk again about the new spec formatting style. Throughout the last two decades, there has been a movement towards "lean and clean" screenwriting: Shorter screenplays, shorter paragraphs, shorter speeches, more white space, and the omission of technical instructions. It should come as no surprise that this gradual evolution continues to refine *spec* style. Let's take a quick look at where things stand at this moment in time.

The technical stuff
Let's start with what's forbidden. Do not write CONTINUED at the top and bottom of each page. Do not write "continuing" as a parenthetical when a character continues his/her dialogue after a paragraph of narrative description. Do not number your scenes.

Avoid camera directions: ANGLE ON, CLOSE ON, POV, PAN, DOLLY WITH, TRUCK, ANOTHER ANGLE, ZOOM, PULL BACK TO REVEAL, ZIP PAN, CRANE SHOT, ECU, WE SEE, and so on. Avoid editing directions: CUT TO, DISSOLVE TO, IRIS, WIPE. Notice that I use the word *avoid*. *Avoid* means to only use a technical direction when absolutely necessary to move the story forward. That's about two or three times in a screenplay. Remember, you are writing the story, not directing the movie.

Parentheticals
You may have read that you should use actor's instructions (parentheticals) sparingly, that you should not direct the actor in saying his/her lines unless the subtext is unclear, and that since executives only read dialogue or just a few pages, that you should include some action as a parenthetical to help improve the read.

Let's be honest, executives are getting younger, often lack a creative background, and are asked to read more. The result is they read less. But readers (professional *story analysts*) read everything, after which they make their recommendation to the executive or producer. It's that recommendation that places your script in the running for a deal.

In view of that, continue to use parentheticals sparingly, but consider taking occasional opportunities to add a line of action (about 3-4 words) as a parenthetical if doing so adds movement to the scene. And don't be afraid to write brief description. Film is still a primarily visual medium.

How lean is lean?
Try to keep your screenplay within 110 pages (120 pages max). Paragraphs of narrative description should not exceed four lines. As a general rule, each paragraph should focus on an image, action, or story beat. Thus, paragraphs will often be only a line or two in length. Dialogue lines should not exceed 3.5 inches in width. Ideally, dialogue should consist of one or two lines, maybe three. (Yes, there are exceptions to everything.)

Author's intrusion and style
Generally, you should stay out of the script. Shane Black made "author's intrusion" hip. Here's just one example from page 91 of *The Last Boy Scout*: "Remember Jimmy's friend Henry, who we met briefly near the opening of the film? Of course you do, you're a highly paid reader or development

executive." Shane Black can get away with that; you and I can't. But having a personal writing style can add a lot to the read. I loved reading *Romancing the Stone*. The first line begins, "A size 16-EE boot kicks through the door...." I came away thinking that Diane Thomas had a lot of fun writing that story. I had a lot of fun reading it.

What *can* I use?
Use the MONTAGE, the SERIES OF SHOTS, the INSERT, the INTERCUT, the FLASHBACK, and SUPERs. Use these for dramatic or comedic purposes (or for clarity or ease of reading), not to dress up the script.

I have a copy of the original *Basic Instinct* spec script by Joe Eszterhas—the one he sold for $3 million. There is not a single DISSOLVE, CUT TO, ANGLE ON, or fancy technique in his entire 107-page script. Only scene headings (slug lines), description, and dialogue—that's it. His focus is on telling a story through clear, lean, unencumbered writing.

The bottom line
Keep in mind that your audience is the reader of your script (as well as movie-goers), and that he/she is weary of reading scripts. So don't encumber his/her read with technical directions. Just let the story flow like a river. That river will flow if you use visual, clear, and concrete language that directs the eye without directing the camera, and touches the heart without dulling the senses.

Finally, don't get paranoid about formatting rules; the story is the thing. Readers don't care if you indent 10 spaces or 12 spaces for dialogue, just so long as it looks "about right," has a clean appearance, and (most importantly) reads well. Hopefully, your lean script will earn you a fat check.

HOW TO TACKLE WRITER'S BLOCK

At last there is hope for suffering writers

originally published in *Script Magazine*
www.scriptmag.com

Few people realize that Writer's Block is a progressive disease that not only attacks the verbal processing lobes of the brain, but also debilitates the emotional response center as well. What starts out as a minor case of *idea retardation* can eventually deteriorate into *acute blithering idiotus*. The final stage of this horrible disease is *anonymity*.

Until recently, there was no hope. Now, recent research has shown that Writer's Block is actually a broad category of many related diseases, each with its own characteristics and symptoms. Identification of these specific diseases (or blocks) has made it possible to find a cure. If you have recently experienced any of the following common symptoms--finger paralysis, plot disorientation, or coagulation of the creative juices--then take heart! Help is here at last.

Autobiographicosis
This is one of the most common of all blocks. What makes this disease so insidious is the victim is often oblivious to the problem until it's too late and the script is rejected. Afterwards, the writer may recall a dull awareness of a flat and lifeless main character, or of a hero who is passive, perfect, and who has become an observer of the events of the screenplay.

At the core of this malady is the writer's past. His writing is so autobiographical that his characters have no life of their own, but have become mere appendages of the writer. As such, they can only act and speak in accordance with the writer's memories.

Once I read a script about a wife who was abused by her husband. The wife did nothing but complain for 90 pages. On page 100 a neighbor rescued her. The only reason I read this all the way through was because I was paid to evaluate it. I thought to myself, "This is often how real people behave, but movie people are willful and active."

The writer had painted herself into a creative corner. She was too close to the truth. She needed to use the energy of her personal experience and create a drama with it. Even "true" stories combine characters and condense time for dramatic purposes. She was suffering from *autobiographicosis.*

The cure for this condition is a radical charactectomy, or removal of the characters from the writer. The result is characters that emerge on the page with a life of their own-- active, imperfect, and volitional. Sure, they may be patterned after aspects of the writer or of the writer's life, but they speak with a voice of their own.

In the early stages of autobiographicosis, the writer can be rehabilitated through a temperance program in which she learns to be close enough to her characters to love them, but distant enough to be objective and creative in her relationship to them.

Scribaphobia
Scribaphobia is characterized by a conscious or unconscious avoidance of writing the script. Writers with this disease would rather do the dishes than face the computer terminal. Often there is an underlying fear of not being equal to the task.

When scribaphobia was first discovered, it was widely thought that it was transmitted through casual contact with a computer diskette or even a keyboard. Now we know that this disorder, like all other blocks, is not communicable. Here's a progressive treatment that has helped thousands overcome the heartbreak of scribaphobia.

First, stop comparing yourself to William Goldman. In fact, don't compare yourself to anyone. You are unique and will make your own unique contribution.

Second, identify your fears about writing and courageously face them off, one by one. They will gradually shrink until you're in total remission.

Third, have a definite writing schedule and commit to it. Force yourself to write. Invariably, the first three pages will be crap, but once they are written, the creative juices will begin to flow.

An athlete never jumps into a major workout or a game without first doing warm-ups to work out the kinks and to prepare the body for optimal performance. Writing is similar. Try a few reps of letter writing to warm-up, or a few laps with a shopping list, or the obligatory three pages of crap already mentioned. Once your mind is warm, it can more easily perform.

Chronic Ambivalence Syndrome and Museheimer's Disease
These two ailments are related because both deal with *toxic befuddlement.*

Chronic ambivalence syndrome (or CAS) is nothing more or less than not knowing what to do next. In many cases, you may not need to know what to do next--just keep writing and trust the process.

However, if you are experiencing a loss of equilibrium, get feedback from a professional. Writing Groups can also help you in talking the writing problem out. Sometimes a seminar or a good writing book will help you gain the perspective and orientation you need.

Museheimer's Disease, on the other hand, is the false belief that there is a Muse assigned specifically to you who will come down from Olympus and whisper in your ear all the action and dialogue for your script. The obvious symptom for this disease is suddenly finding one's self staring at a blank page or computer terminal for hours on end.

The problem here is not the existence or non-existence of the Muse. The problem is trying to write a script from scratch without first creating a premise, designing a core story with plot twists, and developing the characters.

Even then, you should consider outlining the story before you actually sit down to write it. This progressive, therapeutic approach will get you back on course in no time. Remember, you don't have to write the whole screenplay today, just a few pages.

Stuckitis

This is actually an advanced case of chronic ambivalence syndrome where the writer suffering from CAS lapses into a *stuckitic coma*. The way out? Mental concentration. The writer must draw on all her mental and analytical powers in trying to solve the writing problem.

The next step is to relax, wait, and concentrate on something else—badminton, pottery, anything. Meanwhile, the subconscious mind will work on the problem—this is the incubation phase.

It is followed by an *involuntary benign stroke*, an inspiration that usually strikes during a shower, at bedtime, or at some

214 *Dr. Format Answers Your Questions*

other calm moment.

The fourth step is a conscious evaluation or analysis of this offering from the subconscious. Once done, you may continue with your writing project.

Intrusion of the Inner Critic
If you've ever been in a creative fever and then suddenly found yourself correcting spelling and punctuation, then you've experienced this pernicious affliction which has blocked many a creative flow. To understand this disease, you must first understand how the mind works.

The mind has two sides, a creative side and an analytical side. Great writing presupposes the ability to alternate between the two sides. While in the creative mode, often called "writing from the heart," it is important to keep the "head" out of the way. And that's the problem. The analytical side often *intrudes* on the creative side. The cure is to teach this "Inner Critic" to wait its turn.

The key to the cure is to remain relaxed. Just brush these intrusions aside--don't give them a second thought. Tell yourself,

"I don't need to get this right. I just need to get this written. I can evaluate it later."

When creativity fades, many writers induce its return by closing their eyes and visualizing the scene they are writing. Some listen to music. Others take a walk with a note pad. Anything to retain a relaxed but alert state of mind.

Preventive Medicine
Measures can now be taken *before* you are stricken with any of these diseases. First, end any writing session in the middle of something. Hemingway advised, "Leave some water in the

well." By ending in the middle of a scene, paragraph or sentence, you make it easy to get back into the writing flow at the next session.

Second, realize that writer's block is an occupational hazard that every writer faces. When encountering a block, don't panic, just say, "Oh, this is normal, no biggie, I'll just work through it."

Third, trust yourself, trust the creative process within you, and trust the writing tools in your possession. Believe that everything is going to work out fine. Most of all, take the pressure off. Make writing fun, and you'll have fun writing.

INDEX

For information about Dave Trottier's books, freebies, and services:

Master evaluation and consultation
14-point script analysis
Query letter analysis
The Screenwriter's Bible
Updates to *The Screenwriter's Bible*
Online courses
Retreats
Mentoring
Free *Muse*Letter
Free screenwriting information

Visit Dave's web site, or contact him:
www.keepwriting.com
dave@keepwriting.com
1-800-264-4900

For information about *Script* magazine
or to send a question to Dr. Format:

www.scriptmag.com • experts@finaldraft.com
Subscriptions 888/881-5861